Radiohead

the Complete Guide *to their*

BE CHARGED

OMNIBUS PRESS
London/New York
Paris/Sydney/Copenhagen
Berlin/Madrid/Tokyo

D0620560

Mark Paytress

Cover designed by Chloë Alexander

ISBN: 1.84449.507.8
Order No: OP50457

Exclusive Distributors
Music Sales Limited,
8/9 Frith Street,
London W1D 3JB, UK.

Music Sales Corporation,
257 Park Avenue South,
New York, NY 10010, USA.

Macmillan Distribution Services,
53 Park West Drive,
Derrimut, Vic 3030,
Australia.

To the Music Trade only:
Music Sales Limited,
8/9 Frith Street,
London W1D 3JB, UK.

Every effort has been made to trace the copyright holders
of the photographs in this book but one or two were
unreachable. We would be grateful if the photographers
concerned would contact us.

Printed and bound in Great Britain by Mackays of Chatham plc, Chatham Kent

A catalogue record for this book is available from the
British Library.

Visit Omnibus Press on the web at
www.omnibuspress.com

INTRODUCTION

IHEARD IT COUNTLESS TIMES. SO YOU'RE WRITING ABOUT RADIOHEAD? *YOU poor sod!* Whether they love 'em, or whether they loathe 'em, everyone has an opinion on them. And each one of them, whether favourable or critical, begins with the word miserable and ends in despair. But is that really all that can be said about Radiohead, the self-hating offspring of Joy Division's Ian Curtis and suicide chanteuse Nico?

They are an unprepossessing bunch, that's for sure. Neither gothic nor textbook 'dark', yet you wouldn't baulk if they pulled up in a long black limousine and carted a dead relative away. But all that stuff about 'depressing old Radiohead' is nonsense, really. If there was no such rock band (especially one able to command the attention of the world's stages) that still believes in the power of music to do all those things it once claimed to do - now that would be *truly* depressing. Radiohead never boast that what they do might change the world in any significant way (they've never written an 'All You Need Is Love', an 'Anarchy In The UK'). But they're thrillingly aware that, as part of Andrew Loog Oldham's 'industry of human happiness', it is still possible for a bunch of musicians to fly in the face of the philistinism that always seems poised to engulf it (1963, 1974, the entire 1980s, 1995, much of the new century).

Radiohead make music you want to hear again and again. Some claim that makes them *progressive*. They fly in the face of all those dumbed-down cultural cliches: that difficulty is no fun, that elitism is inappropriate, obscurantism too. Why, Radiohead might even still believe in Art! Not that they deliberately go out of their way to be any of these things. They simply refuse to believe that the easy options are always the best ones.

You might think that such lofty ambitions, however unconscious, would be the death of any band, transforming them into a bunch of dreary right-on musos loved by the courtiers but hated by the masses. Well, Radiohead's commercial clout has wobbled a bit of late, but they're hardly cult corner yet. Though that's not to say that as the function and meaning of pop mutates further still, they might yet find their work being wheeled into incinerators by cheerless adults and cheering children.

But far from being harbingers of an even more disturbed future, Radiohead's work is full of optimism because in it we find hope that things don't necessarily need to be this way. Yes, it's full of premonitions, despair at a world that teeters at the edge of self-destruction, and a suspicion that those who live in it are deeply traumatised. But perhaps that is precisely why Radiohead make music of such extraordinary feeling and, lest we forget, beauty. You do wonder whether only those who have glimpsed the abyss are capable of doing so. Whatever it is, it's a rare commodity.

Lighten up. Give this extraordinary body of work a listen.

Mark Paytress, November 2004

THE EARLY YEARS

IN 1993, WHEN RADIOHEAD WERE LITTLE MORE THAN AN ASPIRING, IF RATHER run-of-the-mill indie combo, they possessed two key attributes. One was 'Creep', the slow moving hit single that had tucked itself right behind Nirvana's 'Smells Like Teen Spirit' as the second hymn of the slacker generation. And there was the group's name. "Great connotations," insisted singer Thom Yorke who, like the rest of his colleagues, knew instinctively that Jude, Gravitate, Music and all those other rehearsal-room suggestions lacked gravitas.

It's difficult now to disassociate 'Radiohead' from everything the band, the brand and their music now signifies. Right from the start, though, the name prompted a range of associations, from the oppressive, artful weirdness of David Lynch's *Eraserhead* to vaguely subversive notions concerning the mass media and its audiences. "It's very much about the passive acceptance of your environment," Yorke once claimed, a remarkably prescient assessment given Radiohead's subsequent interest in issues of cultural dissemination, reception and, above all, manipulation.

The significance of the name makes more sense in hindsight. Back in the early Nineties, it was merely one in a long line of snappy, single-word rock monikers, alongside, say, Slowdive and Curve. However, it's worth contemplating its source for a moment, even if it turns out to have come from one of the least memorable songs on one of the least significant albums by New York art-rock luminaries Talking Heads. The title ('Radio Head') may have been inspired, but the song - a cod reggae workout from 1986's *True Stories* – was not. Nevertheless, the association with Talking Heads is apt, as Radiohead guitarist Ed O'Brien has confirmed. "We always felt this massive affinity with them," O'Brien told *MOJO*'s Nick Kent, "because they were white folks grooving in a 'college geeky' way and still making records as good as Al Green."

Whatever else they've achieved since 1993 (and that includes making records every bit the equal of Al Green and Talking Heads), Radiohead have been unable to shake off their reputation as 'geeky white students' who make music for a similar constituency. Coming from Oxford, a city that will remain forever dominated by a centuries-old reputation as a seat of learning, hasn't helped. And neither did the admission that all five once attended Abingdon School, a fee-paying establishment that regarded academic failure as it would an outbreak of leprosy.

Radiohead's distinctly middle-class origins are inescapable, and certainly relevant, though this has often lazily been used as a stick with which to beat the band. That's partly because their emergence coincided with the launch of a rash of 'lads mags' that exploited the crisis in modern masculinity with a faintly queer blend of flesh, fisticuffs and fast cars. While key beneficiaries Britpop rivals Oasis and Blur slugged it out in the tabloids, Radiohead became the darlings of the broadsheets, and were depicted as party-pooping Lord Snootys more inclined to chin-stroking than jaw-bashing. It spoke volumes about the depressing state of class stereotypes in Britain that a gulf once imaginatively flouted by The Beatles' remarkable efflorescence four decades ago now seemed more insurmountable than ever.

If social trends weren't necessarily on their side, Radiohead at least benefited from recent changes in rock's wider mainstream, which had clawed back some dignity after its mid-Eighties torpor. For three decades, the bedroom fantasist had grown up safe in the knowledge that rock'n'roll provided a refuge for the misunderstood, the misfit. All that changed after 1980, after punk had pointed an accusatory finger at a music industry that had grown conceited and coke-fuelled. But far from being dead and buried, rock's old guard regrouped, ushering in a new era of giganticism. As punk's rhetoric faded away, entertainment spectaculars became the order of the day, characterised by military-style organisation and a sea of glowing lighters. Rock had been transformed from freak show to a fireworks-night-with-guitars extravaganza.

This enfeebling process was neatly inscribed on the records of this period. Hip hop and dark corners of the indie sector aside (which you can literally count on the fingers of one hand: Sonic Youth, Big Black, Butthole Surfers, My Bloody Valentine), much of the music of the Eighties still sounds as lame today as it did back then. So much so that conspiracy theorists must wonder whether the new breed of producers were in the pay of the Thatcher and Reagan administrations...

All this makes the emergence of a band such as Radiohead, who epitomise much that runs counter to rock's ra-ra decade, even more remarkable. But just as the band members continue to stay close to their home town, in spite of its suffocating reputation, so too do they enjoy an ambivalent relationship with the era that – despite everything - fired their initial interest in music.

With the exception of guitarist Jonny Greenwood, born in 1971 just as Glam Rock was tarting itself up for the cameras, the members of Radiohead were late Sixties arrivals just old enough to have perceived punk rock as a cartoonish adjunct from their prankish, pre-teen obsessions – naughty though not necessarily liberating. In fact, Thom Yorke's first musical role model was not the rabble-rousing Sex Pistols but a pomp-rock guitarist who more closely resembled a Jacobean royal, Queen's Brian May.

Yorke, a keen cyclist and Lego architect, admitted to being gripped by a "pervading sense of loneliness... since the day (he) was born". Born with a lazy left eye which, despite several operations, proved difficult to rectify, Yorke has insisted that his ocular oddness hadn't resulted in him "getting kicked around" at school. Maybe not, but the cruel taunts of 'Salamander' and suchlike would have left a lasting effect on any child's psyche. Acutely aware of his sense of difference, the 11-year-old Thom Yorke picked up the Spanish guitar he'd owned since his eighth birthday and wrote his first song. He called it 'Mushroom Cloud', though has since insisted that the subject matter was more frivolous than the apocalyptic title suggests...

Inevitably, perhaps, the young teen gravitated towards the music of the post-punk malcontents, most notably Joy Division, whose downbeat, despair-drenched work was given a tragic twist after singer Ian Curtis committed suicide in May 1980. Poised to join cold wave malcontents PiL and Siouxsie And The Banshees in ruffling up the rock mainstream, Joy Division might have made all the difference had they been given the opportunity. Instead, as they mutated into dislocated dance gurus New Order, traditional songwriting enjoyed a renaissance, spearheaded by The Smiths in the UK and R.E.M. in the States. Very soon, the 'anything goes' independent scene that had blossomed in the aftermath of punk began to fade.

The roots of Radiohead can be traced back to the association of 14-year-old Thom Yorke and future Radiohead bassist Colin Greenwood, who bonded over their Joy Division records and a mutual passion for dissident subcultural apparel. With Yorke writing songs, and the classically trained Greenwood on guitar, the pair had their own 'punk' band as early as 1982. TNT was the first of several school combos, among them Shindig, Dearest and Gravitate (yes, that one again), by which time they'd been joined by another guitarist, the lanky, brass-trained Morrissey lookalike and aspiring thespian, Ed O'Brien.

On occasion, this makeshift combo was augmented by an all-girl horn section. More troublesome, though, was finding a reliable backbone to hold it all together. One day, after the group's Boss Dr Rhythm drum-machine broke down, the classically trained Phil Selway stepped into the picture.

Although Radiohead didn't sign a deal until December 1991, their five-piece line-up was already in place as early as 1987, towards the end of their schooldays. By this time known as On A Friday, simply because Friday was rehearsal day, they'd somehow found their ranks swelled by Colin's brother Jonny. Greenwood junior was a good couple of years younger than the rest, and though no one quite knew what role this harmonica-wielding, viola-trained youth would play, no one had the heart to tell him to push off either.

Musically, the nascent Radiohead still had a long way to go. They'd added homegrown acts such as The Cure and The Blue Aeroplanes to their private playlists, though it was the retro-ish sounds of the Paisley Underground emanating out of America that characterised their first demo, six songs recorded on four-track and circulated among friends early in 1987. (Titles included 'Lemming Trail', 'Mountains [On The Move]' and – possibly with a nod to Queen – 'Fat Girls'.) By the time of the second, a 14-tracker, Thom Yorke – his hair now dyed blond in homage to Japan front-man David Sylvian - was even affecting a mild American accent.

Transatlantic in his musical tastes, Thom Yorke nevertheless seemed uncompromisingly parochial when it came to his gap year. There was, one presumes, far too much going on 'inside' for him to join the rest of the flock in fleeing the Oxford borders at the first opportunity. With three band members now scattered across the country at various universities, Yorke's reluctance to leave Oxford meant that On A Friday were able to regroup for the occasional concert. By now, sets would blend a handful of Yorke origi-nals with several covers, including an Americanised version of The Rolling Stones' 'Jumpin' Jack Flash'.

It says much about the group's camaraderie and mutual respect that On A Friday survived this period of dispersion intact, a four-year spell that concluded when Yorke – who resumed his studies a year later than every-one else – completed his Literature and Art degree at Exeter University in summer 1991. Fired up by Sonic Youth, The Pixies ("They were the best band ever," reckoned Ed O'Brien years later), Dinosaur Jr and the first stirrings of the pre-grunge Seattle sound, On A Friday were committed enough to begin serious discussions of a possible career in music as early as 1989.

During his West Country sojourn, Thom Yorke continued to write songs between acquiring an appreciation of the work of Francis Bacon, growing sceptical of the literary canon, and developing an angry aversion to the puke'n'prank rituals of undergraduate life. One day, Colin Greenwood received a cassette from Yorke in the post. Containing an acoustic version of a new song, 'Creep', its arrival had a dramatic effect on Greenwood. "This is my destiny," is how he put it years later.

Yorke's close ties with his fellow Oxford brethren didn't prevent him from moving in new circles while he was away. He DJ'd at college, got into what he later described as "rubbish techno" and found himself a girlfriend (Rachel Owen, now his long-term partner). He also played guitar with the Exeter-based Headless Chickens, whose sets sometimes included a high-speed version of High & Dry – later reworked for *The Bends*. Another song, a polite-punk anthem called 'I Don't Want To Go To Woodstock', was recorded in 1989 for a 1,000-only various artists EP, *Hometown Atrocities*. The track, which also features Yorke on backing vocals, has since been made available on the *Year Zero: The Exeter Punk Scene 1977-2000* compila-tion (Hometown Atrocities).

Shortly afterwards, the group changed its name to Headless (they'd discovered that another Headless Chickens were active in New Zealand), and later, Flickernoise, by which time the group's sound incorporated dance music elements. Yorke's tenure was short-lived, though, and as soon as he completed his studies with a Mac-made on-screen recreation of the Sistene Chapel, he returned to Oxford.

By now, Yorke had forged a strong musical bond with Jonny Greenwood, the latecomer to On A Friday who had recently switched from keyboards to guitar and was experimenting with his own four-track machine. Having three guitarists in the band might normally have seemed excessive, but with the instrument enjoying a renaissance thanks to the blossoming of Nirvana and the dirge-like Seattle sound, the additional fire-power was hardly inappropriate.

Anticipating that Yorke's return would herald a more serious approach to their career, On A Friday recorded a three-song demo in April 1991, the so-called On A Friday Tape. Wedged between the R.E.M.-inspired 'What Is It That You See?' and the dancefloor orientated 'Give It Up' was 'Stop Whispering', a simple but effective song that built unceasingly and caught the ears of many who heard it.

One of those was local producer Chris Hufford, who invited the group to record a second, five-song demo at his own Courtfield Studios. Titled, deceptively, *First Tapes* (alias *The Manic Hedgehog Tape*), this included the live favourite 'Phillipa Chicken', 'Nothing Touches Me' (inspired by an artist imprisoned for child abuse), plus three songs that would reappear on their debut LP, *Pablo Honey*: 'I Can't', 'Thinking About You' and 'You'.

Surprisingly, it was the initial demo - and 'Stop Whispering' in particular - that brought On A Friday to the attention of EMI Records, altering the band's priorities from 'desperately seeking gigs' to 'Do we have enough material for an album?' at an instant. The key moment came when label sales rep Keith Wozencroft walked out of the Oxford branch of Our Price with a copy of the demo tape, thrust into his hands by an opportunist shop assistant, Colin Greenwood. Wozencroft was sufficiently intrigued to catch one of the band's live shows and, impressed with what he saw, brought half of EMI's A&R department with him when he came down a second time.

By November 1991, and with the *Manic Hedgehog* tape in the hands of several record companies, On A Friday found themselves at the centre of a bidding war. Offering the band the security of an eight-album deal (though the label's historic associations with The Beatles no doubt played its part), EMI/Parlophone won out, and a deal was duly signed on December 21, 1991.

Pablo Honey

(Parlophone 0777 7 81409 2 4, February 1993)

ON APRIL 1, 2003, A NEWS STORY WENT UP ON GREENPLASTICTREES.COM, AN unofficial website that nevertheless enjoys a close relationship with the band. According to the report, Radiohead planned to include a newly re-recorded version of Pablo Honey as a bonus disc with the forthcoming Hail To The Thief. It was April Fools' Day, so there was no truth in the story whatsoever. But so much had changed in the intervening decade that the idea contained more than a shred of credibility.

Back in 1992, when Pablo Honey was recorded, mainstream rock was rediscovering its bite. Nirvana's *Nevermind*, an American hardcore version of punk rock with added metal flash, was everywhere. In Britain, too, guitars were making a return: mashed up with baggy beats in 'Madchester', or else lathered in white noise by the FX-obsessed 'shoegazing' bands. A handful of the latter variety, including Ride and Swervedriver, hailed from the Thames Valley area, where they'd been working roughly the same circuit as On A Friday. Except that now, just weeks after inking the Parlophone deal, On A Friday had become Radiohead. And with a three-guitar front line, and their sights set on international success, they looked not to the Thames Valley for inspiration but right across the Atlantic.

The noise coming out of America was clearly more robust than the quaint and floppy-fringed English bands (My Bloody Valentine excepted), most of whom were still hopelessly in thrall to The Smiths-inspired jingle-jangle. *NME*'s Keith Cameron, an early champion of Sub Pop and the so-called Seattle Sound, stumbled upon Radiohead shortly after the name change. "A pitifully lily-livered excuse for a rock'n'roll group," he reckoned, a phrase that apparently haunted Thom Yorke for months afterwards. And for good reason, for the singer knew instinctively that unexceptional Brit-rock fare, pitched some way between U2 and indie orthodoxy, was not the answer to career longevity.

The band's label, Parlophone, were far more forgiving, though even they recognised that the swift change in musical climate necessitated a toughening up of the group's sound. The solution was to team Radiohead with two Boston-based producers, Paul Q Kolderie and Sean Slade, whose track record - The Pixies, Dinosaur Jr and Throwing Muses – certainly impressed the band. After the limited impact of the debut *Drill* EP earlier that spring, Kolderie and Slade joined the band in summer 1992 at the Chipping Norton Studios. Three weeks later, and at a cost of around £100,000, they emerged with the basis for their debut album.

But Kolderie and Slade's job was by no means complete. Returning to their Fort Apache studio near Boston, Massachusetts, to work on the tapes, they found the project "a bit of a struggle", with Kolderie claiming the band baulked at the use of reverb and "wanted to be The Beatles". The results – charitably described in *Melody Maker* as "promisingly imperfect" - suggested that while Radiohead aimed high, they had neither the experience nor the imagination to pull it off. By the standards of the day, *Pablo Honey* isn't a bad record, but its triumphs are minor (such as the application of a certain professional polish), and the results often sound secondhand. The guitars are fashionably loud, the quiet/loud dynamics a transparent debt to Nirvana, The Pixies and the sound of angry young America. Diluting the effect with some U2-like dramatics, and some stale, indie-lite residues didn't necessarily enhance the effect either.

It's no exaggeration to say that one song dominated the album – to the point that it obscured virtually everything else the band did for the next couple of years. Whether touring Britain in the company of forgettable student fare Kingmaker and The Frank And Walters, or spending much of 1993 in the States supporting Belly, James and, bizarrely, Tears For Fears, it was always 'Creep', that irrepressible, hook-filled anthem of alienation, that the crowds had come to hear. The band knew it, and the thrill of knocking out Britain's answer to 'Smells Like Teen Spirit' each night soon wore off.

Yorke, whose pain-wracked lyric was invariably assumed to be autobiographical, suffered most. With the spotlight of transatlantic success leaving him vulnerable and exposed, the singer "hit the self-destruct button pretty quickly". By autumn 1992, he was experiencing stage-fright and, seeking further refuge, had moved out of the band's loosely communal premises into a flat of his own – in a basement, of course. But the self-flagellation didn't end there. The band's star turn was no longer 'Creep' but 'Crap', and in a further twist of self-loathing, Yorke even began to adopt Keith Cameron's "lily-livered" description of the band, seemingly without irony. It was a classic best of/worst of times scenario.

As well as providing a shop window for this ambitious band, *Pablo Honey* also supplied the lump of concrete to toss through it. After first vindicating the group's self-belief, it then rudely shattered it. For, once presented with a magnified version of themselves, Radiohead – and Thom Yorke in particular – were in the grip of the curse of creative progress. Being feted for one lightning bolt of greatness was not, they decided, a legacy but a beginning.

Even the band's indie-drab demeanour became an issue. "Does he have star quality?", asked *Select*'s Andrew Collins in May 1993, shortly after Thom Yorke had disguised his functional crew-cut with some extraordinarily wretched hair extensions that made him look like some mutant son of Ziggy Stardust. "I want nothing more in the whole world than to be a star," the singer replied, perhaps a shade too enthusiastically. "Nothing more," he stressed. "That's it. Period." Despite the healthy half million sales notched up by *Pablo Honey* in the States, and decent chart placings on both sides of the Atlantic, Radiohead's cracked actor was, within months of the record's release, considering a solo career.

Pablo Honey established the band's name, and sold more copies than even Parlophone might have hoped for. And yet it's not remembered with much fondness. Looking back at the record and its times with *MOJO*'s Nick Kent in 2001, Thom Yorke quietly admitted: "I just don't recognise myself at all". To Ed O'Brien, *Pablo Honey* – which took its title from a sketch by New York telephone pranksters The Jerky Boys - was "a collection of our greatest hits as an unsigned... naïve, young, impressionable band". A collection that's still best remembered for *that* hit.

YOU

'YOU' WAS one of four songs from the On A Friday demo tapes deemed fit for inclusion on the debut Radiohead album. The 1991 recording had already enjoyed a repeat airing on *The Drill* EP, the band's May 1992 debut, and though this set opener sticks closely to the original arrangement, this reworked version is beefier and more convincing. Like just about everything else on the record ('Creep' excepted), 'You' is hardly world-changing, or even head-turning for that matter. The dynamics are taut and well-rehearsed, the air is thick with guitars – some chiming, others grinding, soon to become a Radiohead trademark - and Thom Yorke's vocals are more foregrounded. The performance is committed, but the song's best moves sound cliched, giving the impression that 'You' is, essentially, indie angst by numbers. There's a clear trace of Bono-like bluster in Thom Yorke's voice, though more interestingly, he reveals an early tendency to soar in a manner soon to be associated with the up-and-coming American singing genius Jeff Buckley. Appropriately, there's an air of doomed romanticism about the song, fortified by a mildly fucked-up waltz beat and Yorke's lyric ("I can see me drowning/ Caught in the fire"). The singer had, it seems, already found his metier.

CREEP

LONG before it slow-burned its way into 'alternative nation' consciousness, there was something "fucking special" about this song. Written by Thom Yorke while he was at Exeter University (and "in the middle of a really, really serious obsession"), it was sketched out on a tape and mailed back to Oxford for approval, where it found instant favour. His supposed "Scott Walker song" - a reference to its almost celebratory mix of private pain and musical theatrics – 'Creep' had a simple, hypnotising power matched by nothing else in the band's repertoire.

Perversely, the song's conventional structure and killer hook ("I'm a creep/I'm a weirdo") seemed to trouble On A Friday who, affecting a kind of inverted indie snobbery, felt it was all too obvious. Only when 'Creep' received the full soft/loud/soft grunge treatment was the song's potential – and the band's misgivings - finally unlocked. With everything now in place, the only problem was nailing a killer performance, particularly from a group blighted by self-consciousness in the studio.

During a lull in the sessions, producers Kolderie and Slade sensed their moment, nudging the band to 'run through' the song at the Chipping Norton studio where the bulk of the album was recorded. Unfettered by any notions that this was 'the' take, Radiohead delivered as near perfect a version of the song as they'd ever done, something that was confirmed by the spontaneous applause that greeted the end of the song. Aside from some re-cut vocal and bass parts added at a later date, the rest – including that lovely open drum sound – remained as it was originally intended.

Once the basic take was in the bag, both the group and EMI agreed that 'Creep' was the album's obvious flagship single. But there was one problem: that hair-raising reference to being "so fucking special" had to go. Yorke duly obliged, his 'clean edit' now changed to "so very special" for the single release. While in the studio, and at the suggestion of Paul Kolderie, he also reworked the opening verse, losing a reference to a "leg of lamb" in the process.

According to Yorke, 'Creep' had been inspired by "a rocky relationship" with a girl from Oxford's smarter side, a regular on the social scene who favoured a rock venue on Little Clarendon Street over On A Friday's favoured haunt, the Jericho Tavern. But so strong was a generation's identification with the song's self-absorbed air of despair that its genesis now seems almost superfluous. Probably more relevant is an anecdote concerning Jonny Greenwood's 'clunk' guitar that precedes each chorus. "That's the sound of Jonny trying to fuck the song up," reckoned Ed O'Brien, though Thom Yorke remembered it as Greenwood's way of ascertaining whether his instrument was working or not. Either way, these breathtaking interjections - "as ominous as the loading of a rifle", reckoned Mac Randall in his biography, *Exit Music* – provided a perfect motif to illustrate the explosive potential of the 'creep'.

Now one of the key songs of the Nineties, a slacker anthem wedged between Nirvana's 'Smells Like Teen Spirit' and Beck's 'Loser', 'Creep' sold just 6,000 copies when it was first released domestically on single. Abroad, though, it soon found favour in Israel, Spain, Scandinavia and, during winter 1992, in California. News of this success slowly filtered back home, and by the end of the year, 'Creep' figured in the critics' round-up of 1992 highlights. But the song just kept on growing. By the following June, when the band were touring the album in the States, a cheaply produced video was receiving regular plays on MTV's *Beavis & Butthead* show, prompting the song's appearance in the Top 40 and pushing sales of *Pablo Honey* past the half million mark. At the height of 'Creep'-mania, the band's US label, Capitol, organised radio phone-ins where listeners were invited to share their true-life tales of self-loathing in exchange for the chance to win Radiohead T-shirts. This was probably the first evidence that things were already getting out of hand...

No doubt about it: 'Creep' was special. While those other great white hopes back home – notably Oasis and Blur – had been writing songs with one ear cocked to Bolan, Quo and The Kinks, Radiohead had – on this song at least - rejected cosy nostalgia in favour of a homegrown response to the energy and pain of grunge. The only real nod to the past was actually a joke prompted by Ed O'Brien, who noticed that the song's chord progression mirrored The Hollies' 1974 hit, 'The Air That I Breath'. This inspired Yorke to 'quote' The Hollies' melody midway through the song, a falsetto-voiced gesture to another band cursed by the epithet 'unfashionable'.

Like Nirvana's Kurt Cobain, Thom Yorke was soon saddled with the unbearable weight of his work's meaning. "I suppose I asked for it," he admitted later, acknowledging that his "Mr Serious Of Rock" persona had been largely of his own making. But while Yorke has never quite managed to shake off his 'Mr Serious' notoriety, Radiohead soon tired of being 'the Creep band', and eventually dropped the song – Number 1 in the *NME*'s 1993 Readers' Poll – from their live set. It was memorably revived when the group made a triumphant return to Oxford in July 2001, performing in the city's South Park.

HOW DO YOU?

AFTER the skilful explosiveness of 'Creep', 'How Do You?' is a slap in the face, two minutes of punkish posing with Thom Yorke delivering his best gnarly-voiced art school impression (think Magazine's Howard Devoto and Wire's Colin Newman) over a riff vaguely reminiscent of The Stooges' 'No Fun'. There's something of the early Stones here, too, the soapy insistence of 'Stupid Girl' from 1966's *Aftermath*, perhaps. More accurately pinpointed is the snatch of spoken-word material that's buried deep towards the song's end, which is lifted from the same Jerky Boys tape that gave *Pablo Honey* its title.

Lyrically, the song is a bile-filled attack on social inadequates, with Yorke tearing into the "powerful freak", the "dangerous bigot" who's "bitter and twisted" and yet simply "wants to belong". Most damning is the line, "He's just like his daddy", a bleak suggestion that traditional manhood is still a long way down the food chain.

STOP WHISPERING

A SURVIVOR from the first On A Friday demo tape, where it played out with a burst of psychedelia-inspired wah-wah guitar, 'Stop Whispering' was smartened up for the *Pablo Honey* sessions. An integral part of the band's live set, and at five and a half minutes, something of an epic, 'Stop Whispering' was an obvious product of the Velvet Underground school of songwriting. Tough yet tender, it's a two-chord slow-burner that only comes alive towards the end when the guitars diverge, one as if it's playing through a Leslie speaker, Beatles-style, another toying with some exotic Eastern scales.

The limitations of the song neatly mirror the feelings of inadequacy that forms the basis of Yorke's lyric. "I can't find the words/ And I can't find the songs", he wails at one point.

'Stop Whispering' was subsequently remixed and edited by Chris Sheldon – shedding its daring climax - for single release in the States, where it failed to maintain the momentum of 'Creep'.

THINKING ABOUT YOU

L IGHT years away from the musical advances Radiohead would soon become known for, 'Thinking About You' serves to illustrate a point: that beneath all their indie-rock posturing, the band were deadly serious about their craft, just like Costello and U2. In fact, this one virtually comes accompanied by a sea of raised fists and lighters...

'Thinking About You' was another old favourite, having previously appeared in quite different forms on the *Drill* EP and, before that, the *Manic Hedgehog* tape. Here, shorn of its callow, electric energy, the new, pared down arrangement was obviously regarded as evidence of the band's 'maturity', that they were now sufficiently grown up to rip apart their own work and strip it back to its essence. The subject matter, though, remains defiantly adolescent, with Yorke playing the spurned protagonist left masturbating into his own self-pity. Apparently, the song was a favourite of Jonny and Colin Greenwood's mother. "She had no idea it was about wanking," said her younger son.

ANYONE CAN PLAY GUITAR

I N COMMERCIAL terms, this was an obvious follow-up to 'Creep' which, on its original release in September 1992, stalled disappointingly short of a chart placing. Despite its attitude-heavy verses, cliché-ridden chorus and Nirvanalite dynamics, 'Anyone Can Play Guitar' was nevertheless afforded *NME* Single Of The Week status, and only just missed out on a Top 30 chart placing in spring 1993.

In a literal echo of the title, everyone present in the studio – including the female cook – was given a guitar and told to play what they wanted for the intro. Jonny Greenwood wielded a paintbrush artfully, while Thom Yorke (in an echo of Pink Floyd's Syd Barrett) ran a coin down his guitar neck, though the resulting 'chaos' sounded forced and unconvincing.

On the face of it, this joins a long line of homages to the empowering attributes of the six-string ("Anyone can play guitar/And they won't be a nothing any more"). But, remember, this is a Thom Yorke lyric; things aren't always what they seem. While he resists smothering the song in cheap irony, his teeth-baring growl about wanting to "be Jim Morrison" appears to be genuinely iconoclastic. "I just ranted that verse the day after I saw the [Oliver Stone] film," he said. "It really wound me up, really upset me. It was like he was some sort of Arthurian legend or something."

RIPCORD

THE Clash's second album, *Give 'Em Enough Rope*, tailor-made to suit the American market, has a lot to answer for. It marks the moment when punk's songs of rage were given a corny, Springsteen-like dash of showbiz bluster, in turn spawn-

ing an unstoppable genre of overly earnest, preachified, air-punching rock typified by U2, Simple Minds, et al. That pretty much sums up 'Ripcord': pointless rock stodge that seems to serve no other purpose than to irritate the hell out of anyone who still harbours the fantasy that there's more to rock music than foot-tapping and till-rattling.

VEGETABLE

JUST when the album appears to hit rock bottom, up pops this oddly Stones-ish cut (check out the *Exile*-era Keef licks), that starts unpromisingly, redeems itself with a gloriously impassioned chorus - and tosses in an acidic West Coast guitar break for good measure. When Yorke cries, "I'm not a vegetable/I will not control myself", there's a wonderful desperation in his voice that goes that way beyond the rebel yell of the stadium stooge.

PROVE YOURSELF

CREEP' excepted, perhaps the killer chorus of the entire album turns up here on what's otherwise another fairly run-of-the-mill slice of indie orthodoxy. It's surprising, then, that Radiohead chose to launch their career with this song, which opened the *Drill* EP with rather less panache than the version here. The slouching intro, which probably owes a small debt to Dinosaur Jr, is overshadowed by the superbly effective change of pace when the deceptively infectious chorus kicks in. But once again there's something hand-me-down about the song. Even Yorke fails to deliver his oft-repeated hook, "I'm better off dead", with anything like the gravitas Kurt Cobain would to a similarly morbid sentiment. In truth, Yorke's transparently self-pitying lyric is evidence of the song's age, 'Prove Yourself' first being demoed by On A Friday back in 1991.

I CAN'T

THIS ALSO dates from the On A Friday days, and unlike 'Prove Yourself', was deemed important enough to kick off the band's famed *Manic Hedgehog* tape. The version here is one of two album tracks recorded for the album by producer/manager Chris Hufford at Courtyard, then mixed by Paul Kolderie and Sean Slade back at their Fort Apache studio. "I had high hopes for that one and I don't feel like it panned out that well," Kolderie later admitted to *Q* magazine, citing that he would have taken the song at a more accelerated pace. The result was, he declared, "a real nightmare".

Once again, the spectre of The Pixies isn't too far away (especially noticeable towards the song's end), although the track gets underway with a retro-psych guitar line, and also draws on the mid-Sixties for some Mod-style harmonies. Despite the attractive ornamentation scattered through the song, 'Prove Yourself' was busy going nowhere fast. And not too fast either.

LURGEE

STARTING out like an outtake from the Velvet Underground's slothful third album, 'Lurgee' – English slang for disease – meanders trance-like, owing much to the band's early inspiration, R.E.M., masters of the bewitching guitar jangle. Lyrically, too, the song is sparse, with Yorke's occasional utterances reflecting a desire for strength as another relationship comes to an end. 'Lurgee' was the second of two songs taped by the band at Courtyard with Chris Hufford at the controls.

BLOW OUT

INDIE mush production cliches aside, there's much to commend this sprawling album closer, which starts out in a light, (Love's) *Forever Changes* vein (with shades of Simon & Garfunkel in the vocal interplay), before switching into Sonic Youth mode, complete with overamped guitars and howling feedback. In letting loose their musical abilities over jazz-tinged elegance and detuned guitar disturbance, Radiohead unveiled a depth to their work that wasn't always apparent on the rest of the album. In keeping with the song's sense of abandon, Yorke allows his miserabilism to hit new heights, his stretched, theatrical utterances transforming self-pity into a comforting new aesthetic. "Everything I touch turns to stone," he sings repeatedly, delicately, and – so observers might have been forgiven for thinking – with some pre-science. For despite 'Creep', despite a few rare moments of sonic irides-cence, there was little to suggest that *Pablo Honey* contained even a germ of imminent greatness. By the standards of the day, it was well played and well made. But by the standards we've come to associate with Radiohead, it was, well, all fairly forgettable.

The Bends

(Parlophone 7243 8 29626 2 5, April 1995)

THERE'S **A LONG ESTABLISHED TRADITION WHERE A KILLER DEBUT ALBUM** (The Rolling Stones, The Velvet Underground, The Pink Floyd, Patti Smith, et al) is invariably followed by... more of the same. Sometime during the Eighties, when rock's rulebook – and, disappointingly, most of its glory – was discarded, all that began to change. Bands like Sonic Youth, The Butthole Surfers and, back home, My Bloody Valentine, entered with a way-out whimper before genuinely hitting their stride two, three, sometimes four albums later. That, too, has been the Radiohead approach. Maybe there's a better, simpler analogy: in Beatles terms, if Pablo Honey was 1963 and Please Please Me; The Bends fast-tracked to 1966 and Revolver.

The Bends was the band's first post-fame album, conceived, more or less, as a complete entity from start to finish. The record took a giant step that seemed to mock the cosy parochialism of the emerging Britpop pack, and provided the perfect riposte to those who had predicted that 'the Creep band' would soon be consigned to the dustbin of history. In fact, while most eyes were trained on Britpop's battle of the egos – Blur versus 'Quoasis' - Radiohead concentrated their efforts on their work, and how to transcend the dumbed-down and retro nature of the so-called indie sector.

Radiohead refused to lie back and think of Little England. Tortured by the staggering response to 'Creep' at the expense of the rest of their work, the band determined to free themselves from its spectre and instead fashion a new *raison d'etre*. It didn't come easy: there were three producers, all of whose efforts were once again fed into a mixing-desk across the Atlantic, three recording studios, numerous false starts and agonising debates over musical direction. Worse still, having dined well on the fruits of the group's initial success – both in terms of ego-boost and lifestyle - Thom Yorke briefly harboured fantasies of breaking free completely and forging his own solo career.

As the group's frontman, chief songwriter and Angstmeister-General – not forgetting the day-to-day responsibilities of simply being Thom Yorke - he'd had a remarkably difficult 1993. Inevitably, much of this found its way onto *The Bends* which, he admitted later, had been "an incredibly personal album, which is why when it came out I spent most of my time denying it was personal at all". As early as August 1993, the band had been forced to pull out of a prestigious appearance at the Reading Festival. Publicly, the reason given was that Yorke's voice had gone – the result of a constant cycle of tours, rehearsals and publicity drives. Privately, those close to the band knew that Yorke was simply too exhausted to perform.

Back home in Oxford, Thom Yorke fretted about his future, channelling his anxiety into a new cycle of material. By Christmas, he'd assembled enough material to fill a cassette with some 23 songs in various states of progress. Having resolved his dilemma, Yorke was back with Radiohead by the start of the new year, and rehearsing in a soundproofed shed on an old fruit farm near Didcot. A producer, John Leckie, had been earmarked to work on the second album the previous summer, by virtue of his impressive track record – he'd previously worked with Radiohead faves Magazine, The Fall, The Stone Roses and psych-spoof XTC spin-off, The Dukes Of Stratosfear. But with the sessions continually delayed, the producer first had to perform production duties for fellow Thames Valley student faves Ride before he could switch his attentions to Parlophone's brightest hopes.

By the time Leckie was free to join them at RAK Studios in North London, Radiohead had virtually rehearsed themselves into the ground. The veteran producer had a remedy. On the first day of the sessions, on February 28, 1994, he brought in a copy of the John Lennon/Plastic Ono Band album, the ex-Beatle's remarkably stark – both sonically and emotionally – plea for simplicity, and sanity. (The young Leckie had been tape operator during the sessions.) While the producer has since recalled that Yorke was probably more "stunned" by the Tom Waits album he also played that day, there's a sense of purpose, righteousness even, about the Lennon set that seemed to sink deep into the Radiohead psyche from this moment on. Initially, that roughly translated itself as knowing what they didn't want, rather than knowing what they wanted. But in time, some of Lennon's rejuvenated sense of self-belief began to kick in.

The first couple of months at RAK were awful. The record company's initial demand for a late spring single, followed by an album in October, raised the stakes - and the temperature in the studio. "A total fucking meltdown for two fucking months," Yorke complained after the album's release. Part of the problem was having too much material to work with. In fact, several songs were at some time considered as the follow-up to 'Creep''s second-time-around success the previous autumn, including 'The Bends', 'Sulk' and '(Nice Dream)', as well as 'Killer Cars', which ended up on a B-side. The major sticking point, though, was getting 'a sound', prompting much discussion of amps, guitars and production techniques.

By April, and with sessions "all a bit too manic", according to Leckie, they decided to shelve the single idea. Instead, with just a palmful of songs to show for their efforts thus far – including 'Fake Plastic Trees', 'Just', 'Planet Telex', 'Black Star', 'Street Spirit' and a partially completed 'My Iron Lung' – Radiohead packed up and took off on a three-month tour of Europe, the Far East and Australia.

Despite the graft - and John Leckie clearly remembers Thom Yorke sat at his piano promptly at 9am every day, six days a week – and modest results, the sessions taught the band an important lesson. From this point on, they'd learnt to consider the studio itself as an integral part of the creative process. Both Leckie – "like a caring uncle" said Yorke later – and RAK in-house engineer Nigel Godrich were crucial in this respect, the former demystifying the role of the producer, and the latter (who'd simultaneously been working on Scott Walker's spellbinding *Tilt* project), increasingly tempted into greater risk-taking.

When Jonny Greenwood later asserted that Radiohead had "recorded 40 minutes of accidents... and called it *The Bends*," this acknowledges the key role that spontaneity played during the protracted sessions. But acknowledging the accidental is not to be confused with improvisation, for the truth is that much of the material that made it onto *The Bends* had been road-tested on tour in summer 1994.

The Radiohead that turned up at The Manor studio for a couple of weeks later that summer was a quite different beast to the dazed and confused animal that had left RAK in the spring. Buoyed by the creative leaps and bounds taken in the recent shows, they now attacked the new material with vigour and imagination. Having completed work on *The Bends* at Abbey Road in the autumn, Radiohead were then told that the results weren't American enough and, citing the relative failure of 'My Iron Lung', the first single from the sessions, EMI once again had Sean Slade and Paul Kolderie finesse the material.

Everyone waited with baited breath, though "the finished product was a lot harder than I imagined", admitted John Leckie, sentiments echoed by Jonny Greenwood, who was simply relieved that "it doesn't sound like Simple Minds". Thom Yorke just beamed from ear to ear. "It's great," he told anyone within earshot. "It's got 12 versions of 'Creep' on it."

The band's confidence in the new material was such that Thom Yorke and Jonny Greenwood began to perform acoustically from late '94 well into 1995. And when *The Bends* appeared that April, their new-found self-belief was justified by the almost universally positive reviews that greeted the album. "A majestically desperate record," purred *Q* magazine; the rest queued up to stand in line. The domestic market was now willing to embrace Radiohead, recognising their remarkable advance with a Number 6 chart placing. Across the Atlantic, though, America struggled in vain to locate another 'Creep', let alone a dozen of them, and quietly ignored the vastly improved band. (*The Bends* first secured a miserable Number 147 chart placing, though after further touring, the album eventually crawled up to 88 during 1996.)

Watching the band from the wings during Radiohead's support slot on R.E.M.'s Monster tour of 1995, Michael Stipe admitted: "Radiohead are so good they scare me". It was true. While no one could miss the occasional lapse into R.E.M./U2 grandiosity, 'Radiohead' had now developed their own signature, and *The Bends* possessed a genuine sense of ambition that belied the record's emergence during the nostalgia-drenched post-Nirvana rock world. With the cautious approach of *Pablo Honey* now all but erased, and a dramatic new song, 'Subterranean Homesick Alien' already a regular in the set, Radiohead were now poised to tip the balance firmly away from convention towards invention.

PLANET TELEX

COMPARED with this, everything that Radiohead had previously recorded sounded like the work of impressionable teenagers – which wasn't too far from the truth. 'Planet Telex' marked the arrival of a bigger, badder sound, and a band no longer shackled to rock cliché or a safety-first approach to finding recognition. Pitting a weary, only vaguely coherent Thom Yorke against a heavy, John Bonham-style backbeat, 'Planet Telex' was a far cry from the three-guitar attack of the previous album, instantly erasing any assumption that Radiohead were a "lily-livered excuse for a rock band". Apparently recording his vocal at four in the morning, his head on the studio floor after a wine-filled night in a Greek restaurant in Camden, Yorke admitted: "I was bent double and I hadn't got a clue what I was singing." This was the true, disorientating sound of intoxication and displacement. The success of *Pablo Honey*, and especially 'Creep', had airlifted Radiohead out of the pacific English countryside and into a check-in, check-out lifestyle, feted on world-famous stages, fussed over in hotel din-ingrooms and more confused than they ever were.

It's that whirlwind transformation that informs 'Planet Telex'. (Its original title, 'Planet Xerox', would have been more fitting but the photocopying giant vetoed its use.) "We did it on the spot," producer John Leckie told *Q* magazine, remembering its genesis at an early session in RAK Studios. Frustrated by their inability to nail a song, the band adjourned to a nearby restaurant. After a generous helping of food and booze, they returned buzzing with a novel idea – to create a new song out of an old one. Taking the electric version of 'Killer Cars', recorded at RAK in January (and later issued on a B-side), they isolated the drum track, created three individual samples and 'stitched' them together. Yorke sat at his Yamaha piano and bashed out some heavy-handed chords which, run through a delay unit, tickled and teased the unyielding, mechanistic percussive thump. With the addition of a robust bassline and some goth-lite guitar chords, Yorke then delivered the performance of his career, his frustrated, hand-wringing lyric a perfect mate for the tension-filled sonics going on all around him.

Partly emancipated from his conscious self, Yorke found that his vocals now sounded more convincing than ever. It was as if all that earnest endeavour involved in songwriting and performance had been lifted, allowing some hitherto unidentified force to take control. The opening line declares as much: "You can force it but it will not come." Yorke - and Radiohead - had unwittingly made their first genuine move into sound as an abstract concept, and the newly depersonalised lyrics (best exemplified by the repeated "Everything is broken" quip) marks a significant advance too. No wonder the group chose this instinctive leap of musical confidence – sketched out over dinner, executed almost immediately in a boozy studio session - as the album's opener.

THE BENDS

IF THE weird, wonderfully assured rhythms of 'Planet Telex' set the record's new-found confident tone, it was by no means indicative of a complete turnaround in style. In fact, there is something reassuringly old-school about the grand manner in which the title track announces itself, with a strutting, Seventies AOR power-chord riff. *The Bends* was the second oldest song on the record, having been written and demoed on four-track by Thom Yorke during sessions for *Pablo Honey*. Perfected in concert long before the album sessions, the song was nailed in a single take at The Manor in summer 1994. Apparently, drummer Phil Selway had been keen to get off and do a bit of property viewing.

The bombastic three-guitar assault, and the song's more conventional structure, betrays *The Bends'* vintage. But with more air in the production and Thom Yorke's fabulously flamboyant delivery – with discernible overtones of Dylan, Bolan, Bono, Ray Davies and punk rock – the song transcends its rock band blather and succeeds thanks to its taut arrangement and neatly nuanced progression.

The song itself was reminiscent of Queen, Television and, most obviously The Beatles (Yorke's apparently ironic "I wish it was the Sixties" jibe pastiched Lennon on 'I Am The Walrus'), though what pulls it together is Yorke's lyric. In a single performance, he embodies all the alienation, doubt and paranoia that lies at the heart of the band's work. "Where do we go from here?" he starts, drawing both on his personal and professional life. The band "don't have any real friends", the singer's "words are coming out all weird". And Thom Yorke is enduring debilitating bouts of paranoia ("They brought in the CIA, the tanks and the whole marines to blow me away"). No surprises, then, given the song – and album – title. 'The bends' refers to an agonising condition prompted by deep sea divers surfacing too quickly, and the record is shot through with medical references. Jonny Greenwood had recently noticed that his singer's onstage antics had lately resembled someone "desperately trying to wriggle out of his body", a peculiarity alarmingly reminiscent of Joy Division's Ian Curtis.

Weak/strong, and possibly ill from the intense scrutiny that came with fame and the expectations it creates, Yorke remained self-absorbed and "so fucking special" in classic frontman fashion. But despite writing this at the outset of his public career, he hadn't totally trashed the unfashionable notion of humility, as his concluding "I want to be part of the human race" attests. He was already keenly attuned to the power and function of music, too. Hearing a marching children's band (complete with barking instructor) from his hotel window in Arizona, he reached for his cassette recorder, and a snippet from this introduces the song, subtle evidence of Yorke's growing politicisation.

But did he really wish it was still the Sixties? "Levi's jeans might wish it was," he said later. "I certainly fucking don't."

HIGH AND DRY

WHILE at Abbey Road working on 'Sulk', one of the last songs to be cut for the album, the band rediscovered this, taped a year earlier at Courtyard Studios, during the spring 1993 sessions for the 'Pop Is Dead' single. The performance was loose (live sound engineer Jim Warren was at the controls), and after much jesting that the song's

gentle style owed something to Rod Stewart ('Maggie May') or Paul McCartney ('Mull Of Kintyre'), the band quickly forgot about it. A&R man Keith Wozencroft hadn't, and he dug the recording out for John Leckie to hear, prompting the band to reassess the song once unceremoniously dubbed "fucking dreadful" by Thom Yorke. Deciding that everything was already there on the original take, 'High And Dry' was tweaked at the production stage by Slade and Kolderie and, suitably rehabilitated, it became the second single from the album, peaking at Number 17 in spring 1994 just as *The Bends* hit the shops.

The lyric's jaundiced take on fame ("You're turning into something you're not") sounded like more self-flagellation on the part of the 'Creep' who'd made good, but Yorke had written the song during his days as a student at Exeter University. He'd performed it on stage with the Headless Chickens, though On A Friday shunned it, suggesting that Yorke's doubts concerning its appropriateness for Radiohead were deep-seated.

FAKE PLASTIC TREES

AFTER his traumatic 1993, Thom Yorke had banished all thoughts of going solo. But this, recorded a year after his 'wobble', was the closest he'd come to a solo performance thus far in the band's career.

The basis for 'Fake Plastic Trees' was laid down in a traumatic session the night after Radiohead had witnessed a spellbinding Jeff Buckley performance at the Garage in North London on September 1, 1994. The song itself had been inspired after a week's overload of fake plasticity in Los Angeles, a bitterly tragicomic scenario about which Yorke later revealed, "I wrote those words and laughed". Delivering them was another matter entirely. After completing the third take, Yorke, accompanying himself on acoustic guitar, broke down and cried. And that, microphone crackle and all, was the version John Leckie had been waiting for.

The performance – for which Yorke hit some Jeff Buckley-style falsetto notes – had been difficult enough. Building an arrangement around it proved "a fucking nightmare", said the singer. With string players John Matthias (violin/viola, ex-Headless Chickens) and Caroline Lavelle (cello) booked in to play their parts, Jonny Greenwood wrote a hasty score, which he based on the romantic style of 20TH century American composer Samuel Barber. It was largely in vain, for Slade and Kolderie later mixed that element of the song right out. More clearly noticeable was Greenwood's own organ part (played on the Abbey Road Hammond which, so they whispered, had once been used by John Lennon), which added a melancholy Bad Seeds vibe. Though the rest of the group made telling contributions towards the end of the song, 'Fake Plastic Trees' was essentially Yorke's show. Once this

track was in the bag, he finally felt he'd begun to crack the finer art of songwriting.

BONES

THIS was taped at The Manor Studios, shortly after the group had returned from their Far East tour of June 1994, and on the same day that the title track was nailed. "Easily the best day of recording," reckoned Jonny Greewood, though in truth, neither track proved to be an album highlight.

Bones doesn't begin too promisingly, its mullet rock backbeat hardly suggestive of anything extraordinary on the horizon. All comes good on the chorus, though, which erupts out of nowhere. Yorke yelps in the manner of Suede's Brett Anderson, while the flamboyant, rock'n'roll guitars riff madly like Ziggy-era Mick Ronson. Some of the success of this supercharged moment must be credited to Slade and Kolderie, who returned to their work with The Pixies for inspiration while mixing the song. Radiohead were reportedly delighted with the results.

The original version of Bones, as recorded during the drawn-out RAK sessions, was well over a minute longer, thanks to Jonny Greenwood's elongated ending, which had been something of a personal homage to The Fall. But when the band took the song on the road, the arrangement was tightened up, thus providing the template for the final studio take.

(NICE DREAM)

THOM YORKE turned to his sub-conscious night-time reveries for inspiration on this song written during the *Pablo Honey* sessions. Placing the title in parenthesis was an all-too-obvious suggestion that this particular dream had been somewhat less sweet, the cue for Jonny's Greenwood to rudely inter-rupt the song's breezy waltz-time reverie with a brief outburst of menacing guitar. "There was a great danger of it being too airy-fairy," Yorke explained. "We wanted it to sound a bit sinister." But he was less than happy when the band began to tinker with other aspects of the song, taking particular offence at Jonny's arpeggio intro (although Yorke later claimed it was one of his favourite moments in the song). Matthias and Lavelle's strings are a little more audible this time, like-wise some whale noises (taped in an aquarium by John Leckie), which surface at the end of the guitar break. Most endearing of all, per-haps, is the Abba-styled call and response interplay between Yorke and Ed O'Brien towards the end of the song.

The singer once claimed that '(Nice Dream)' was somehow linked to Kurt Vonnegut's *Cat's Cradle*, a 1963 novel that finds both rational science and mysticism wanting. Though no one's quite figured out how yet, the theme certainly fits Yorke's world-view.

JUST

THE spectre of Suede's shake appeal returned for this hyper-active song, crammed with all sorts of chords and structural surprises, evidence of Jonny Greenwood's fearsome advances in his attitude to composition. The main guitar motif was pleasingly reminiscent of John McGeoch's majestic, spiralling riff which powered Magazine's 'Shot By Both Sides' into the singles charts back in 1978, though here it's neatly complemented by what can only be regarded as smooth jazz licks tucked in behind the verses. It's very much a guitarist's track, with Greenwood wrenching all manner of exciting sounds from his instru-ment, even hitting a fine streak of white noise towards the end, before playing out with an extraordinary Keef-like break over the oddly funky fade-out.

The other hook was, of course, Thom Yorke's goading "You do it to yourself/You do", a curt, exemplary example of self-loathing. By now, his tortured movements were as familiar as his funboy-free reputa-tion, a trivial assumption based on the melancholia of his songs, the solemnity of his interviews and the tortured soul poses he invariably adopted for publicity photos. But Jonny Greenwood's comment that Yorke's on-stage movements reminded him of someone who's trying to wriggle out of his own skin are entirely appropriate here – and on the promo video that accompa-nies the song, when it became the fourth single from the album, earning a surprise Top 20 placing despite its complicated construction. The song had a third hook, too, the brief pause right after Greenwood's first solo, which announces the imminent return of the chorus.

When Radiohead completed work on 'Just' at RAK, it marked the moment when everyone felt the album sessions were truly under way. However, that didn't stop them returning several mixes to Slade and Kolderie before they were happy that the production had been nailed satisfactorily.

MY IRON LUNG

THE FIRST official release since the success of *Pablo Honey* and 'Creep', 'My Iron Lung' – written midway through another gruelling tour late in 1993 - was first attempted at RAK early in 1994 though no one was particularly pleased with the results. A solution came later that spring when, on May 27, an MTV crew filmed the band's Astoria show in central London for future broadcast. John Leckie was on hand to record the performance, and soon noticed that the version of 'My Iron Lung' eclipsed anything they'd come up with in the studio.

After removing most traces of audience ambience, and recording a new vocal track, 'My Iron Lung' was issued on 45 in September 1993 to a mixed response. It hit Number 24 in the UK and flopped in the US completely, but that's hardly surprising as it's not an easy listen. The song's

verses might be gentle, soporific even, but Yorke's delivery is virtually catatonic, a zombie response to months of touring, of having his ego alternately nourished and assaulted. His cynicism is clearly evident, clearly sighing at one point, "We are losing it, can't you tell?" The obvious suggestion is that 'Creep' is the 'iron lung' that keeps the band alive, eclipsing all else - including this, the latest Radiohead recording, as the song so bitterly concludes: "This is our new song/Just like the last one/A total waste of time."

'My Iron Lung' isn't one of Radiohead's most original recordings, the instant recognition of its opening guitar phrase the likely result of one too many nights in with The Beatles' 'White Album', and 'Dear Prudence' in particular. The atonal tantrum that intermittently shatters the song's apparent serenity was far too close to Nirvana's 'Heart-Shaped Box' for comfort, though probably deliberately so in order to affront all that "Radiohead are the new Nirvana" hype. A strange move at the time, 'My Iron Lung' nevertheless proved cathartic, not least because its angular art-rock intent marked a significant break from everything that *Pablo Honey* represented.

BULLETPROOF... I WISH I WAS

THIS song was recorded one lazy Sunday afternoon at The Manor studio in the Oxfordshire countryside - and it sounds like it. A slow,

Pink Floyd-style pastoral, based around acoustic guitar and gentle ambient sounds, its blissful mood belies the sentiment, which was quite clearly zonked-out on-the-road fatigue. The basis of the song – the fourth acoustic-led number on the album – was initially laid down by Thom Yorke, Colin Greenwood and Phil Selway, leaving Jonny Greenwood and Ed O'Brien to work out their own roles. And that's when they came up with the idea of playing through echo units, running cigarette lighters up the fretboard and other Floydian trickery. In order to accentuate the song's out-of-sortsness, John Leckie suggested that they play out of sync with the backing track, which they duly did. The results lend an airy feel to a lyric that reeks of claustrophobia. Later, the band fretted that the song was "a bit slow and timid", though Thom Yorke started telling everyone it was his favourite song on the album. That is, until they recorded the next one...

BLACK STAR

A HASTILY worked-up kitchen sink drama, recorded towards the end of the RAK sessions while John Leckie was busy elsewhere, 'Black Star' has subtle charms that belie it being one of the album's more conventional songs. The fade-in was hailed as an unusual twist (though to anyone with a half-decent record collection, it was hardly *that* unusual); the guitar sound that underscores the verses evokes those lazy,

Let It Be-era Beatles; and the beat comes straight off the debut Breeders album. And once again, what could easily have been dismissed as filler is rescued by a killer chorus, in much the same, seemingly effortless way that *Slider*-era T. A Rex kept the heat turned up.

If the song's quiet serenity was pleasing, and its chorus subtley rousing, it was undermined by a decidedly trad-rock bridge and a hackneyed "Ah, this is killing me" climax. No wonder that Jonny Greenwood later described the song - recorded at RAK and with the studio's in-house engineer Nigel Godrich at the controls – as a piece of "teacher's away larkiness". Yorke's favourite bit turned out to be Greenwood's subtle guitar rise towards the chorus – which the rest of the group thought was a mess.

SULK

'S ULK' was another early Thom Yorke song, written in the aftermath of the Hungerford massacre in August 1987, when gunman Michael Ryan shot dead 16 people before turning his gun on himself. But by the time the song was completed, at Abbey Road at the end of the sessions in November 1994, Yorke had changed the key, incriminating phrase ("Just shoot your gun") to "You'll never change", a move apparently inspired by the recent suicide of Nirvana's Kurt Cobain.

Though perhaps the weakest track on the album, 'Sulk' took a

Blond Ambition: celebrating their 'Creep'-prompted success the
Radiohead way, late 1993. Left to right, Phil Selway, Jonny Greenwood,
Colin Greenwood, Thom Yorke, Ed O'Brien. *(George Chin/Redferns)*

Playing the chords of fame: Thom Yorke, 1993. *(LFI)*

Pablo Honey (1993).

Having withdrawn from the 1993 Reading Festival due to "exhaustion", Thom Yorke was in better shape when the band played there the following August Bank Holiday. *(Brian Rasic/Rex Features)*

The Bends was the product of countless protracted studio sessions – and it showed. *(Derek Ridgers/LFI)*

Performing on *Later With Jools Holland*, BBC Television Centre, London, May 27, 1995. *(Andre Csillag/Rex Features)*

The Bends (1995).

November 1995: Messrs. Selway, Greenwood, Yorke, O'Brien and Greenwood appear coolly indifferent to the hype surrounding Britpop, then at its peak. *(Gie Knaeps/LFI)*

Down by the water: Thom Yorke takes a between-gig breather, June 1997. *(Mike Diver/LFI)*

OK Computer (1997).

Subterranean homesick aliens: the band off-duty in New York, December 1997. *(Kevin Mazur/LFI)*

Radiohead, 1997: post-*OK Computer*, the biggest band in the world contemplate how to disappear completely. *(Roger Sargent/Rex Features)*

Another night's happy-clappy music, live at London's Brixton Academy, September 13, 1997. *(Ilpo Musto/LFI)*

Thom Yorke shares the stage with Michael Stipe at the Free Tibet concert in Washington, June 14, 1998. "Radiohead are so good they scare me," admitted the R.E.M. singer a few years earlier. But that didn't prevent him from duetting with Yorke on a version of 'Lucky'. *(Kevin Mazur/LFI)*

Live in Frejus, France, June 17, 2000. After undergoing a radical change in direction, Radiohead previewed much of their new electronic-based material in concert prior to the release of *Kid A*. At this particular show, the group premiered the title track. *(LFI)*

Thom Yorke belts out another punchdrunk lovesick singalong, live in Toronto, Canada, October 17, 2000. *(TS/Keystone USA/Rex Features)*

The Octave Doctor: Jonny Greenwood live on stage in Victoria Park, East London, September 2000. *(Brian Rasic/Rex Features)*

Kid A (2000).

What does the future hold? As the group enter a critical new phase in their musical development,Thom Yorke obligingly volunteers his palms for inspection. *(Brad Miller/Retna)*

while to get right in the studio. When the band first tried it out, at RAK in February 1994, the song was actually being considered as a possible follow-up to 'Creep'. And before they finally nailed it at Abbey Road, with Thom Yorke recording his vocal while floored by a stomach bug picked up in Mexico, they'd also tried it out at The Manor without much success. The loping guitar motif that surges into overload during the break is the song's strongest point, though Phil Selway's jazz-inspired drum pattern chips away happily at the group's rockist tendencies. But, pitched somewhere between U2 and the Manic Street Preachers' as yet unveiled 'A Design For Life', the song's simple anthemic platitudes are further exposed by the quality of the song that follows it.

STREET SPIRIT (FADE OUT)

IT WOZ the arpeggio that dun it! After the relative comedown of the previous two tracks, *The Bends* makes a magnificent U-turn in the nick of time with this remarkable pay-off piece. This was as far from the jaw-jutting clichés of the emerging Britpop as anyone could possibly imagine, a magnificent example of the redemptive power of music, a transcendent moment of minor key magic that – though we didn't know it then – was to point the way forward. Incredibly, at a time when artful subtlety and pop chart success appeared to be as estranged as ever, 'Street Spirit'

became the fifth single from the album, and secured a Number 5 placing, Radiohead's best yet.

Ed O'Brien's bittersweet arpeggios, which weave around a subtle, spacious rhythm track, contribute much to the hypnotic, meditative power of a song that, after so much bluster and bile before it, makes a final, beautiful peace with the melancholic disposition. Tension does inhabit the song, though it's blissfully restrained in the manner of Otis Redding's similarly insistent 'Try A Little Tenderness'. But instead of opting, like Otis does, for the grand climactic exorcism, Radiohead gently raise the tempo, bring on a small string section, and - teasingly – suggest a fade-out (as per the song title) before instead bringing the song to a quiet, dignified halt. Apocalypse rock ("Scream as they fight for life" indeed) has never sounded so serene.

OK Computer

(Parlophone 7243 8 55229 2 5; June 1997)

THE IDEA, RECKONED THOM YORKE, WAS TO MAKE A RECORD THAT WAS BOTH cool and yet easy to listen to while eating. "We could fall back on just doing another moribund, miserable, morbid and negative record," he added, shortly after *The Bends'* release, "but I really don't want to." It was some hope. The moment the singer began to note down any positive thoughts, his head was flooded with what he called "mental chatter". His struggle for serenity in a world where fatally flawed social structures were propped up by a seductive, drip-fed hyperreality invariably supplied him with far more scope for Radiohead's next, eagerly anticipated album.

A rare instance of a contemporary record daring to take on the big issues of its time, *OK Computer* was instantly acclaimed as a key rock music landmark, a *Sgt Pepper* for the net generation, a richly textured slice of art-rock that both embodied its times and transcended them. Perched precariously, yet somehow perfectly, between art and commerce, between analogue and digital, between modern and postmodern, between crisis and comfort, between music and all else that lies beyond it, *OK Computer* showed what happens when worlds collide.

While accidents were by now integral to the Radiohead methodology, there appeared to be nothing unplanned about the record's scope and ambition, which had even the most jaded critics struggling to find new superlatives. Perhaps most remarkable of all was how the band took the mainstream indie-rock audience with them, away from the trad-rock song structures that had dominated since the early Eighties towards a new radical fusion of prog-rock and avant-punk.

While *The Bends* revealed that much progress had been made since the indie-rock orthodoxy of *Pablo Honey*, there was little to suggest that Radiohead would cross another major threshold for a second consecutive time. The secret of modern-day fame, after all, was to find a winning formula and – give or take a few superficial tweaks for the sake of novelty – stick to it. But Thom Yorke had been shuffling the cards in Brian Eno's pack of Oblique Strategies, taking particular note of the one that instructed, "Whatever worked last time, never do it again". And so, piqued by the progress they'd already made, Radiohead set out determined to put imagination before consolidation.

Self-sufficiency was crucial to their requirements, so they despatched engineer – and from this point on, co-producer - Nigel Godrich with instructions to build a studio. Several weeks - and £100,000 – later, Radiohead had their own state-of-the-art converted apple shed in the Oxfordshire countryside, which they duly dubbed Canned Applause.

The band spent much of January and February 1996 at the new studio with Godrich, who'd already been road-tested on the new, post-*Bends* song, 'Lucky', installed as their producer. The new, not-too-far-from-home surroundings proved conducive to work, too. For by the time Radiohead took off in March for yet another American tour, several new songs had all been worked up, almost all eagerly installed into the live set. Among these were 'Subterranean Homesick Alien', 'Let Down', 'Electioneering' and 'No Surprises', virtually the backbone for *OK Computer*.

As with *The Bends*, work on the album was fitted around the constant touring schedules – and Radiohead were back in the States in August supporting Alanis Morissette. But this time there was also their leap-in-the-dark attitude towards their work to contend with. For now, more than ever before, Radiohead were extending their collective palette. For Thom Yorke, it was the metronomic rhythms of early seventies Krautrock. Jonny Greenwood bought himself a vintage, Theremin-like instrument called the Ondes Martenot. The others too searched for new perspectives on their instruments, bassist Colin Greenwood even squeezing in a round of private lessons between tours.

Having returned to Canned Applause during May and July, Radiohead broke out later that summer. Hiring St Catherine's Court, a stately residence near Bath owned by the famously fragrant actress, Jane Seymour, they set up their equipment in the magnificent 15th century ballroom. Alternating between mansion and converted apple shed, they emerged some time around Christmas 1996 with something approaching a finished album.

Various string parts were added at Abbey Road in the New Year, and during the first few months of 1997, the finished material was mixed at several locations. (For old times' sake, Slade and Kolderie were asked to remix a couple of tracks, but their efforts went unused.) Sequencing the record proved no less difficult than any other stage in its making, Thom Yorke shuffling endlessly with the songs on his MiniDisc, until hitting on the perfect combination of pace and thematic consistency. (His MiniDisc also proved useful for grabbing various 'slice of life' sounds heard on his travels, some of which were dropped into the album.

The blissful melancholia of 'Street Spirit', which closed *The Bends*, had dramatically signposted the future. And that was the mood maintained on Radiohead's first official post-*Bends* releases: 'Lucky', issued on *Help!*, a fundraising compilation, in September 1995, and 'Exit Music', recorded for the soundtrack to the 1996 film, William Shakespeare's *Romeo + Juliet*. But it was when the band opted to release a six-minute-plus epic as their first proper single in over a year, in May 1997, that the scale of Radiohead's latest achievement began to unfold.

The labyrinthine course of 'Paranoid Android' prompted the inevitable accusations of prog rockery, forcing Yorke to counter that while he'd been listening to the music of the progressive rock dinosaurs, he thought it was "all awful". More pertinently, during the making of *OK Computer*, he said he'd been playing The Beatles' 'White Album' and Miles Davis's *Bitches Brew* ("A record for the end of the world," he proudly declared). "You aim for these things," Yorke told band biographer Mac Randall, "and end up with your own version." There's little doubt, though, that the Fender Rhodes piano which was all over the album had been inspired by Davis's extraordinary late Sixties work.

Further background influences, Yorke claimed, had been *The Tibetan Book Of The Dead* and assorted literature on the Situationists and the student riots in Paris, May 1968.

The singer was rather more vague when it came to possible meanings that might be drawn from the record. "It's not really about computers," he said, but the "noise that was going on in my head... mental chatter" aroused by travel, telephones, television, and virtually everything else in the inescapable contemporary soundscape. That gave carte blanche for all manner of interpretations. Not since *Sgt Pepper* or Pink Floyd's *The Dark Side Of The Moon*, had a record been so thoroughly deconstructed, scrupulously scrutinised for secret 'codes' to crack. Yet from its title in, *OK Computer* was always suggestive, rarely emphatic. However, one thing was certain. The album's kaleidoscopic character was a far cry from the transparently self-obsessed songs on *Pablo Honey*.

"Journalists like it, which is always ominous," Jonny Greenwood told Mac Randall during the four-day media circus that descended on Barcelona for the launch of *OK Computer* in May 1997. No less worrying was the news that the band's American outlet, Capitol Records, had denounced the record as "commercial suicide", and had instantly cut their order from two million copies to a paltry half-million. Happily, they were proved wrong when, after topping the chart at home and debuting at an impressive 21 in the States, *OK Computer* proved that it was still possible to make a record that sounded like no other and yet still reap the commercial reward.

That summer, Radiohead made a triumphant return to Glastonbury, their Saturday night show on the Pyramid Stage now regarded as one of the long-running festival's all-time highlights. Shortly afterwards, the readers of *Q* magazine voted *OK Computer* the best album of all time, a remarkable feat for a contemporary record. The jury might still be out on that one, but certainly the rock mainstream had not been blessed with an album this radical since... Patti Smith's *Horses*, perhaps? Compared to Radiohead's achievement, Nirvana's *Nevermind*, that other great overground/underground rock album from the Nineties, sounds one-dimensional and ordinary.

AIRBAG

WHILE superficially similar to the rhythmically terse 'Planet Telex', which opened *The Bends*, 'Airbag' was a dizzying sonic sculpture. Motored by a looped three-second drum sample, and augmented by dub-wise bass that evoked Jah Wobble's work on PiL's similarly spatial *Metal Box*, 'Airbag' instantly places *OK Computer* in an alternative musical sphere where all divisions between rock and dance music have fallen away. Thom Yorke's vocal, ruminating on car crashes and how to survive them, is disarmingly elegant; likewise, an intermittent guitar posing as a balalaika. The total effect is heady and disorientating, hence the accusations of progressive rock. While it's true that 'Airbag' – originally performed acoustically and titled 'An Airbag Saved My Life' - has something in common with the dark, claustrophobic ultra-prog of Van Der Graaf Generator, its fragmented beats are closer to DJ Shadow or Aphex Twin. When, midway through the sessions, Colin Greenwood was asked what to expect from the new album, his "stoned Radiohead" quip wasn't too wide of the mark on this evidence.

Yorke, who takes great satisfaction in his work once the agony of creation is over, soon revealed his delight in the familiar manner, declaring 'Airbag' as his favourite track on the album. In fact, he'd recognised its worth right away, calling his girlfriend after completing one last, incredibly loud final mix of the song and exclaiming, "We've done something really great" down the phone.

Attempting to explain the meaning of the lyric to *Q*'s Phil Sutcliffe, the singer returned to more familiar terrain. It was, he said, "more about the idea that whenever you go out on the road you could be killed... (and) about how the way I've been brought up and most of us are brought up, we are never given time to think about our own deaths."

PARANOID ANDROID

THE cardinal rule laid down by punk rock in the late Seventies and which, more or less, has been slavishly adhered to ever since is that no pop song need ever extend it welcome longer than three minutes. 'Paranoid Android' brilliantly explodes that notion, and for that and several other reasons, remains one of the cornerstones of the Radiohead catalogue. Clocking in at almost six-and-a-half minutes, the recorded version had been significantly abbreviated since the Alanis Morissette tour, when it featured a lengthy instrumental play-out based around Jonny Greenwood's Hammond organ. More shocking still is the song's constantly shifting structure, quicksilver dynamics and intermittent eruptions of sound - fast becoming a Radiohead trademark – that again sounded distinctly more Van Der Graaf than Nirvana.

In fact, while The Beatles' 'Happiness Is A Warm Gun' (from the *White Album*) is widely acknowledged as the inspiration for the song's labyrinthine, three-part format, 'Paranoid Android' could just as easily be regarded as a younger, more compact cousin to VDGG's 20-minute epic, 'A Plague Of Lighthouse-Keepers'. Many other names have been dropped into the inspirational mix at various times, including Queen's similarly tangential 'Bohemian Rhapsody', Ennio Morricone, Can and the omnipresent Pixies and DJ Shadow. And yet unlike so much deliberate conspicuous sourcing, 'Paranoid Android' – like so much of Radiohead's work – leaves virtually no obvious trace of its genesis behind.

Remarkably, the song, titled after Marvin The Paranoid Android, the boorish robot in Douglas Adams' *Hitchhiker's Guide To The Galaxy*, gave the band a Top 3 hit. Not since those heady hippie days had such a mind-blowing, convention-defying song – in the vein of The Beach Boys' 'Good Vibrations', and The Beatles' 'Strawberry Fields Forever' – been merrily embraced by a mainstream audience. The vibe, though, is significantly less love-filled. "Basically it's just about chaos, chaos, utter fucking chaos," explained Yorke, playing down the barely concealed aggression and misanthropy in his lyric. The most cited evidence of that, the reference to the "kicking, squealing Gucci little piggy", came to Yorke in a bar in Los Angeles, as he wryly observed a

bunch of coke-fuelled smart-asses going about their business. Acutely uncomfortable surrounded by all that well-heeled, self-satisfied 'glamour', he retreated to his room, where he spent a sweat-filled night haunted by what he'd witnessed, worst of all the look in one woman's eye after someone had spilled a drink on her. The spectacle inspired some positively Robespierre-like fantasies ("When I am king you will be first against the wall", "Off with his head"), before his lone-wolf lyric veers off to invoke some natural catastrophe, closing with a deliciously ironic "God loves his children, yeah!"

SUBTERRANEAN HOMESICK ALIEN

DESPITE its blissful air, the sentiments of this song more neatly fit its original title, 'Uptight'. Continuing his assault on the spiritually bereft facts of contemporary life, Yorke has described the song as inspired by aliens "pissing themselves laughing at how humans go about their daily business." Clearly siding with the visitors, the character in the song hopes they'll "swoop down in a country lane", take him away and show him the world "as I'd love to see it". Characteristically happy/sad, the song's despair is obscured by an enchanting arrangement and fantastic imagery, richly evocative of the wide-angled melancholy of Jeff Buckley's father Tim. Another beautiful and shockingly gifted happy/ sad troubadour,

Tim Buckley had died tragically young, an event strangely mirrored when his son drowned in an accident in May 1997, just prior to the release of *OK Computer*.

Continuing with the song's folkish associations, the title was clearly drawn from 1965 Bob Dylan's stream-of-consciousness epic, 'Subterranean Homesick Blues'. In fact, when it was first performed in 1995, 'Subterranean Homesick Alien' featured just Thom Yorke and Jonny Greenwood on acoustic guitars. But when work on *OK Computer* had begun in earnest, Yorke's head was filled with Miles Davis's genre-busting *Bitches Brew*, "nauseating chaos" he reckoned on first listen, before admitting it had been "at the core of what we were trying to do". That probably explains how 'Subterranean Homesick Alien', one of the first tracks to be completed for the album, was transformed from a song into an incantation. Yorke's Fender Rhodes is heavily reverbed in classic late Sixties Davis fashion, while Greenwood – who wrote the intro and the chorus - follows suit with some mellifluous guitar lines.

EXIT MUSIC (FOR A FILM)

IF THIS song feels like a parting gesture, then that's because it was conceived that way – as the playout music for Baz Luhrmann's 1996 film version of William Shakespeare's *Romeo + Juliet*. But it was more, much more than that. For while a second contribution, 'Talk Show Host', appears on the film's soundtrack CD, Radiohead declined to give permission for the producers to use 'Exit Music', claiming the song was "too personal". And unlike 'Talk Show Host', which had already appeared on the B-side of the 'Street Spirit' single, 'Exit Music' had yet to form part of the official Radiohead canon.

"The song is written for two people who should run away before all the bad stuff starts," Yorke later explained, hinting at past hurts. He'd also viewed a 30-minute rough cut of the film for inspiration, and drew on his memories of Franco Zeffirelli's hippie-era telling of the story, which he saw as a 13-year-old, and was struck by the obvious on-screen charms of Olivia Hussey as Juliet. The main ingredient, though, is Thom Yorke himself, whose resigned vocal brilliantly foreshadows the mood of impending tragedy. Biographer James Doheny describes the voice as having a "tomb-like ambience", taped, appropriately enough given her penchant for historical roles, in the courtyard of Jane Seymour's mansion.

It's odd, then, that 'Exit Music' begins in the manner of a late Sixties Johnny Cash song, with Yorke accompanying himself on acoustic. And stranger still that the bleak, fateful mood is intensified by fuzzed-up bass (the ghost of Soft Machine's Hugh Hopper, perhaps), and some shrill, Ennio Morricone-inspired guitar lines. Suitably twisted by a range of disparate influences, the song passes over to the other side with a parting, "We hope that you choke", repeated with cracked conviction. Yorke was dead pleased. "Every note of it made my head spin," he later said.

LET DOWN

THE SHORT silence between 'Exit Music' and 'Let Down', up there alongside many other wonderfilled moments on *OK Computer*, was proof that Radiohead were close to mastering the fine art of sequencing. The mysterious spell of silence is touchingly broken with a perfectly poised guitar arpeggio, Jonny Greenwood's homage both to 'the Spector Sound' and Lou Reed's spidery notes that dart in and out of The Velvet Underground's 'All Tomorrow's Parties'. Both the song's motor and its heart-rending motif, the deliciously delicate notes sweeten the disappointment inherent in Yorke's lyric, and neatly captures the oddly serene sense of helplessness that invariably accompanies a long journey, clearly the song's subtext. "'Let Down' is about what speed and movement do to someone's mind... when you're staring out of a window in a moving train for an hour. All those people, cars and houses passing by," Jonny Greenwood later confirmed.

The song's sparkly light-headedness, neatly undermined by some of Yorke's most arresting imagery ("People clinging on to bottles", "Crushed like a bug in the ground", "Wings twitch, legs are going"), was eventually committed to tape one night in St Catherine's Court at 3am, a suitably magical time to nail what's undoubtedly one of the band's most enchanting, and oddly underrated songs. Things might have been different if the song had been issued as a single, as once planned, but after commissioning a costly video, the idea was shelved.

Midway through the song, Yorke pleads, "Don't get sentimental, it always ends up drivel". It's an observation that sounds wonderfully perverse given that 'Let Down' is probably the most elegant, hearttugging performance Radiohead had yet recorded.

KARMA POLICE

HAVING spent most of his life raging against all manner of machines, as well as bullies and undergraduates, ignoramuses and indie-kids, Thom Yorke was soon disappointed to discover that life at the centre of the culture industries was no less creep-free. Already infamous for shunning the coke, canapes and champagne circuit that keeps the music industry up all night, Radiohead didn't suffer fools gladly. Undesirables penetrating their privacy invariably prompted mock-desperate cries for the "karma police". It was Ed O'Brien who first suggested turning the catchphrase into a song, and Thom Yorke who seemed to find the whole idea funnier than everybody else.

The track's musical backbone came from a well-trod historical source, The Beatles' 'White Album', and one track in particular, 'Sexy Sadie'. There were fewer laughs here, for the song had once made such a profound impression on Charles Manson (of 'The Manson Murders' infamy) that he renamed Susan Atkins, one of his murderous 'lady lieutenants', 'Sadie'. The spectre of Manson, who often spoke of "levelling the karma" of the straight society he despised, seems to infect the song, from the otherwise amusing "arrest this man" hook, to the clearly sinister "This is what you'll get if you mess with us". While there's no evidence that Yorke consciously drew on Manson for inspiration, references to Hitler and the "For a minute there, I lost myself" pay-off also carry eerie echoes of the notorious 'pig' nemesis who is forever irrevocably associated with the 'White Album'.

The second single lifted from the album, 'Karma Police' reached Number 8 in autumn 1997.

FITTER HAPPIER

THE THIRST for list-making in rock journalism has now reached such proportions that we've even been distracted by guides such as 'The Most Skipped Tracks On An Album'. Invariably, 'Fitter Happier', the pivotal piece on OK Computer – and perhaps the ultimate, dehumanised source of its meaning - finds its way onto those lists every time. Given that the track itself is an imaginary two-minute 'wish-list' sketched out by the typical, mildly affluent Westerner, that's hardly inappropriate.

'Fitter Happier' was the only product of an otherwise barren three months when Thom Yorke found himself unable to write anything but lists. Basically a broadsheet supplement's survivors' kit to contemporary living, the lyric consists of 50 'wishes' covering a range of 'issues' – from health and practical concerns to morality and spiritual matters. Idly running his checklist of desires through SimpleText on his Apple Mac computer, Yorke inadvertently found a way to salvage something from his period of writer's block. Utilising the machine's 'voice' to deliver the lyric also freed him from the prospect of him having to sing such goal-driven subject matter straight-faced.

The effect was so compelling/annoying that the subtle backdrop of meandering piano doodles and ominous patchwork of strings, loops and samples – including one from the 1974 film, The Flight Of The Condor - is virtually ignored. Yorke, nevertheless was delighted by the outcome, describing 'Fitter Happier' as "the most upsetting thing I've ever written". Using technology commonly regarded as emotionally blank, he'd succeeded in bringing the lyric to life "in a fucking eerie way". And have 'someone else' deliver a deliciously hideous sideswipe at the hidden cost of capitalism's 'I want' culture, which was the purpose of the "pig in a cage on antibiotics" pay-off.

The 'Fitter Happier' monologue

thrilled some, infuriated most. It also prompted many people to assume that *OK Computer* had been endorsed by high-profile philosopher/scientist Steven Hawking, who famously 'speaks' utilising similar technology.

ELECTIONEERING

LEADING neatly on from the automaton despair of 'Fitter Happier' this, Radiohead's first overtly political song, is vaguely reminiscent of late Seventies agit-prop mavericks The Pop Group. As its title suggests, 'Electioneering' casts a cynical eye over how no one, least of all politicians, are able to stem the trickle-down greed peddled by the multinational corporations.

Yorke was moved to write this unsophisticated yet necessarily savage diatribe against "bullshit economies" and the politicians that prop them up after reading Will Hutton's *The State We're In*, and *The Age Of Extremes*, a Marxist's view of 20th Century history written by Eric Hobsbawm. "I was completely fucking ignorant until I read those," he told *Time Out*'s Pete Paphides. Elsewhere, he has admitted to a prior knowledge of the work of Noam Chomsky, and has also said that the song's fury was also inspired by memories of the Poll Tax riots of 1990.

Many rock musicians, especially over the past couple of decades, have worn their (invariably leftish) political colours in various shades of fashionable pastel. But not Yorke, whose conversion to political activism appears, like Lennon's, to have been motivated as much by an angry, disbelieving idealism as by private club liberalism. And like the 'revolutionary' ex-Beatle, he too tends towards a more apocalyptic vision of the new world order.

This early, unrefined intervention into politically charged rock channels that anger with what sounds like direct action. His cynicism plainly evident in slogan-like lyrics ("Say the right things when electioneering", "I trust I can rely on your vote"), Yorke's rant is neatly complemented by some of the most reductionist riffery Radiohead have ever set down on tape. 'Electioneering' is nothing less than the foul-mouthed gatecrasher at a sophisticated party, and not even the inventive, '68-era Macca-style bassline played on a Novation Bass Station synth can dress up the song – a live favourite around this time - in any other way.

CLIMBING UP THE WALLS

FROM *10 Rillington Place* to *The Honeymoon Killers*, murder most foul – which most of us know only through films - moves slowly. And so it is with this pathologically inclined slice of doom rock, which begins with an institutionalised echo and climaxes in a string-induced cacophony of white noise. "Frightening music," admitted Jonny Greenwood.

Thom Yorke, who gives the song his most sinister performance yet, agreed. "This is about the unspeakable," he explained, meaning the seemingly irreversible increase in mass murderers at large. Declaring that he once worked in a mental hospital when the controversial Care In The Community initiative was introduced, he added that the decision to put mentally unstable patients back on the streets – and thus relieve the state of added financial burden - was hardly care at all. "It's one of the scariest things to happen in this country, because a lot of them weren't just harmless."

His heavily treated voice, which at times sounds so claustrophobic as to be inside the listener's own head, enhances the overriding mood of paranoia, which grows to head-beating, claustrophobic proportions by the song's end. "Some people can't sleep with the curtains open in case they see the eyes they imagine in their heads every night burning through the glass," Yorke further explained. "This song is about the cupboard monster."

NO SURPRISES

FROM the terror-filled 'Climbing Up The Walls' to the childlike bliss of 'No Surprises' might seem a difficult journey to those who like their rock music confined to well-defined spaces, but Radiohead were by now becoming old hands in the ancient art of provocative juxtaposition. And besides, the lines between the two extremes are invariably more blurred than pop-

vox assertions suggest.

Thom Yorke was keen to dismiss claims that 'No Surprises' was in fact a suicide song. "We wanted it to sound like (Louis Armstrong's) 'What A Wonderful World' and Marvin Gaye," he said. "It's the sound of newly fitted double glazing - all hopeful, clean and secure." On the face of it, with Ed O'Brien's shimmering guitar line mimicking Jonny Greenwood's lullaby-like glockenspiel part, 'No Surprises' is innocence personified. But like a Douglas Sirk melodrama, it takes more than the shiny surfaces of modern domesticity ("Such a pretty house/And such a pretty garden") to keep darkness at bay, something confirmed by Thom Yorke's opening words, "A heart that's full up like a landfill". A few lines later, he's reaching for "a handshake of carbon monoxide", forcing the child's music box effect of the lead instruments to take on more sinister tones.

'No Surprises' was the first song to be recorded in the band's new Canned Applause studio, and the version used for the album was the first take, despite several attempts to improve on it. Originally written while touring with R.E.M. in August 1995 ("Colin goes nuts," wrote Yorke in his tour diary after unveiling the song backstage before the group's show in Oslo), 'No Surprises' was publicly premiered that December, a version that was considerably more downbeat than the one here. Apparently inspired by Sparklehorse's 'Sad And Beautiful World', the studio take comes off sounding like the weirdly smiling offspring of The Beach Boys' 'Wouldn't It Be Nice' and The Velvet Underground's 'Sunday Morning'.

The third and final single from *OK Computer*, 'No Surprises' stalled at Number 3 in the UK, a couple of places short of the Parlophone MD's expectations, but still impressive given that the album had been selling like mad for months.

LUCKY

IF 'STREET SPIRIT' had suggested a sophisticated new musical future, then 'Lucky', the band's first high profile post-*Bends* release, confirmed it. They had been toying with the song for weeks when, late in August 1995, Brian Eno's War Child charity, set up to send aid to the children of war-torn Bosnia, asked if the band had a song to contribute to a forthcoming fundraising album. Although their demands ran counter to the Radiohead way of working – all material had to be recorded on one day, Monday September 4, so that a finished album could hit the shops the following Saturday – the group accepted, passing the test in ways even they'd never imagined.

"'Lucky' is a song of complete release," Yorke later told *NME*, adding that it was the first in what he envisioned as a long line of 'happy' material. But while the band managed to throw caution to the wind for the five-hour recording session, Yorke's opening salvo – "I'm on a roll this time/I feel my luck could change" – was hardly an emphatic declaration of levity. It was more like a moment's fanciful suggestion that life need not always be so problematic. Certainly, the procrastination they faced while making *The Bends* had been unblocked, albeit briefly. But Yorke's conversion into a smiley happy person was tentative, to say the least.

'Lucky' starts out like Neil Young's 'Heart Of Gold', before growing into a man-sized epic of early Seventies symphonic rock proportions, complete with sampled choir. Yet it originated in some spontaneously strummed notes by Ed O'Brien while the group were on tour in Japan. "I remember fiddling around [during] the soundcheck," he recalled, "putting together a different pedal order, and actually hitting the strings above the nut on the headstock. It was one of those moments." Not least because the sound reverberated via his delay pedal, thus lending the song its space-rock intro and its dreamy, Floyd-like ambience. Sophisticated and sonically spacious, 'Lucky' was, said Thom Yorke, "the first mark on the wall" that would become *OK Computer*.

THE TOURIST

HAD THIS been released in the Seventies, it would have been cited – alongside Nico's classic 'The End' - as a prime example of Mandrax-gripped musical torpor. And listlessness was indeed Jonny Greenwood's intention, having been inspired to write the music while watching a group of American tourists 'do' the sights of a beautiful French town "in ten minutes". 'The Tourist' is a song about speed," he confirmed, "about the amount of speed you live your life with." Like so many songs put forward for inclusion on albums, Greenwood imagined that his rare musical contribution would end up as a B-side at best. But, as the last song recorded at the *OK Computer* sessions, his weary hymn to drowsiness ("Idiot, slow down, slow down," choruses Yorke) virtually selected itself as the album's closer.

Once again, the spectre of Pink Floyd isn't far away, with Greenwood's Gilmour-like guitar trills sounding spectacularly pre-punk, especially when set against a sleepy waltz-beat that could have been plucked from any early Seventies Grateful Dead album. The whole thing gives off the air of being recorded in an early morning mist, with even Thom Yorke barely able to remember adding his contribution, delivered for guide purposes only and with "no emotional involvement in it". And yet, in the tradition of the finest soul singers, something pure, spiritual even, seems to find an outlet from his exhausted body, a necessary catharsis at the end of an extraordinarily fertile period in the band's career. For, as MOJO's Nick Kent later asserted, *OK Computer* was the record that made Radiohead "the most important rock band in the world".

Kid A

(Parlophone 7243 5 29590 2 0, October 2000)

INTERNATIONAL SUPERSTARS TAKING MUSICAL LEFT-TURNS MIDWAY THROUGH
their careers isn't entirely unheard of. The Beatles wiped the lysergic
smile from *Sgt Pepper*'s face with the sprawling, often downright awkward
The Beatles' 'White Album'. In 1973, David Bowie packed away his Ziggy
regalia in order to create a 1984-inspired musical dystopia, the dashingly
difficult *Diamond Dogs*. And in the early Nineties, Nirvana attempted a
boisterous exit from centre-stage with the Steve Albini-produced *In Utero*.
In 1997, the global success of *OK Computer* put Thom Yorke and Radiohead
in a unique position. They could relax, and go through the motions, merely
tinkering with the façade, like their stadium rock contemporaries. Or,
newly installed as rock's premier frontiersmen, they could continue
developing the Radiohead sound into something even more complex and
challenging. Or they could simply 'rip it up and start again'. In the mind of
their restless frontman, there was only one option...

From decidedly orthodox beginnings, Radiohead had radicalised with
age, taking a sizeable chunk of the rock market with them. The enormous
success of *OK Computer*, and the two years spent touring it – and themselves - into the ground, had put them on the same commercial level as their
teenage heroes R.E.M. and U2. But Yorke, and to some extent Jonny
Greenwood, had been fatally bitten by the bug of musical inquisitiveness. In
an astonishing reversal of the commerce over art conundrum, which had
seen rock follow rather than lead the marketplace since the early Eighties,
an important decision was made. The incremental changes that had seen
the group transform from an Oxford bar band to the most distinctive rock
band in the world would be very deliberately interrupted. And if that meant
they'd very soon fall from grace as a stadium band, then so be it. Some
things, after all, were more important than commercial considerations.

A year after *Kid A*'s release, Thom Yorke told *Mojo*'s Nick Kent that
claims that it had been "intentionally difficult" and an act of "commercial
suicide" had left him in "a state of deep shock. If *Kid A* is difficult," he added,
"then there really is no fucking hope for us." Yorke was talking from the
vantage point of having seen the album top the charts on both sides of the
Atlantic, and thus was feeling mightily exonerated. He virtually repeated
the claim in 2003 when recalling the making of the album for *Q*
magazine's Radiohead special. "All the good bits were done very quickly
indeed," he insisted. "It was just the gaps in between that were long". But
Yorke was also clearly playing politics with aesthetics. For so traumatic was
the making of *Kid A* that for much of its three-year incubation, neither he

nor the rest of the band knew where they were taking the project, or if they'd ever finish it.

It wasn't long after the release of *OK Computer* before Yorke realised that a clear change of course was required. Five days, in fact. Undergoing something akin to an out-of-body experience at Radiohead's huge outdoor show in Dublin on June 21, 1997, he spent his recovery dwelling on a few simple words: How To Disappear Completely And Never Be Found. The pressure-cooker atmosphere of live performance, combined with the exposed nature of public endeavour, was once again playing havoc with Yorke's psyche. Although he recovered well enough to front a historic show at Glastonbury a week later, life on the front-line was becoming increasingly fraught. On November 19, after playing the Birmingham NEC, Yorke was stilled by a sudden paralysis. "I knew people were speaking to me, but I couldn't hear them," he remembered. "And I couldn't talk. I had just so had enough."

When the video diary of the seemingly never-ending *OK Computer* tour appeared, it was titled, with typical irony, *Meeting People Is Easy*. It was, Yorke insisted, "a rough guide on reasons not to be in a band". So by the time Radiohead regrouped for rehearsals towards the end of 1998, the key player was virtually gasping for a change. In one particularly candid scene from the video, he turns to Jonny Greenwood and says: "Last year we were the most hyped band. We were Number 1 in all the polls. And it's all bollocks. Everything's changed. It's just a complete mind-fuck."

Thom Yorke hadn't disappeared completely. He hadn't been allowed to. Besides, it would have felt like he was giving in to forces beyond his control; becoming another Syd Barrett didn't suit him at all. Instead, he did what he always did when the going got tough: lost himself in music. Not those old Smiths and Pixies and U2 and Queen classics. Nor those Krautrock textures that had inspired parts of *OK Computer*. He turned to the sampledelic sounds of contemporary electronica; Auteche, Aphex Twin and Boards Of Canada, all affiliates of the Sheffield-based Warp label. He continued to feast on jazz, the freer the better. Guitar bands rarely got a look-in. Meanwhile, Jonny Greenwood's classical inclinations had led him to the high modernist work of the 20th century Polish composer Krzysztof Penderecki. The spectre of John Lennon stripping himself bare on his 1970 *Plastic Ono Band* LP was never far away either.

During 1999 and into 2000, Radiohead embarked upon perhaps the most radical course of deconstruction witnessed beyond the cosy confines of a Cultural Studies seminar. The rock group that had created *OK Computer*, that had earned all those 'best band in the world' plaudits, had been dismantled. The earliest sessions resembled the first days of school. In one corner lurked Thom Yorke, forever banging on about Pro-Tools, how melodies made him embarrassed, and playing snatches of disjointed rhythms and weird-sounding samples on his new laptop. Grouped together looking perplexed were Phil Selway, closet soul boy Colin Greenwood and Ed O'Brien, who'd been anticipating a return to three-minute pop songs after the excesses of *OK Computer*. Once in a while, Jonny Greenwood peered out from behind his floppy fringe in a bid to piece the various perspectives together.

Meeting people hadn't been easy, but for Thom Yorke, who remained in a state of paralysis long after the NEC show, neither was solitude. "New Year's Eve '98 was one of the lowest points in my life," he admitted to *Q*'s David Cavanagh. "I felt like I was going fucking crazy. Every time I picked up a guitar I just got the horrors. I would start writing a song, stop after 16 bars, hide it away in a drawer, look at it again, tear it up, destroy it... I was sinking down and down... I'd completely had it with melody. I just wanted rhythm." And so, having installed themselves in the Guillaume Tell Studios near Paris, where they stayed for the first few weeks of 1999, Radiohead "changed the methodology", as Ed O'Brien later put it.

Essentially, O'Brien continued, that meant "splitting the band up and reforming it with the same five members". Forcibly detached from their usual instruments, the flustered five quickly found themselves with dozens of new musical ideas, but little idea about what to do with them. Phil Selway remembered the Paris sessions as a time for "tripping ourselves up"; Ed O'Brien reckoned it "a very scary thing". "Bloody difficult," was producer Nigel Godrich's assessment in *Spin*, "Thom really wanted to try and do *everything* different." Still basking in the glory of finding themselves described as the most creative major rock band in the world, the members of Radiohead were now being asked to relinquish their status and start again from scratch. As Ed O'Brien told *Q*, the task now was to learn "how to be a participant in a song without actually playing a note".

The band had road-tested several new songs during their extensive *OK Computer* tour. Tracks such as 'Life In A Glasshouse', 'I Will', 'I Promise', 'Follow Me Around', 'Never Be Found' and 'Nude' (alias 'Big Ideas') were all in various states of completion, and it's a measure of the band's indecision that none would end up on *Kid A*. One of the first songs they tried out in Paris was a particularly ethereal piece called' Lost At Sea'. "Everyone was saying, 'Well, we've got to start somewhere,' remembered Thom Yorke. "But I was standing there, going, 'Yeah, but not here'. Then they'd go, 'So where, then?' And I'd reply, 'I don't know'." It wasn't the best of omens.

Eventually, it was decided that a change of location might help, and the band were packed off to Copenhagen, where they spent a quarrelsome two weeks in Medley Studios. Filling several reels of tape, mostly unusable, they left with around 30-minutes' worth of half-finished material, among them 'Morning Bell', plus the basis of several songs that would later appear on *Amnesiac*.

In April, the band began working at Batsford Park, a 19th century manor house in the Cotswolds, and later that spring it was announced that they'd amassed some 60 songs or fragments of songs. In truth, the most awaited record in the business was a "total fucking mess", Thom Yorke later admitted, and with various insecurities increasingly revealing themselves, more summit meetings were hastily convened. In a vain attempt to instil some order, Yorke – who, uncharacteristically, had been unwilling to explain his new lyrics - chalked up around 50 song titles on a board, but that only intimidated everyone further. One day, Ed O'Brien was spotted holding a guitar. "Oooh, that's strange," remembered Phil Selway, surprised to see such an archaic piece of equipment. "We are essentially in limbo," O'Brien admitted in his online diary, a description already being earmarked as a title for one of the unfinished recordings.

Decamping to Radiohead's newly equipped studio in Sutton Courtenay provided a tonic, and by September 3, Ed O'Brien's online diary – which was now showing considerable enthusiasm for the project – was reporting that the new material was heavily influenced by old school hip hop, funk and soul records. A month later, news emerged that around half a dozen songs had been completed, but by the end of the year, the story hadn't changed. But at last there was some hard evidence; on December 9, a webcast from the band's Oxfordshire studio included a live version of 'Knives Out'. (Typically, when the album finally appeared, 'Knives Out' wasn't on it.)

When the band reconvened after the Christmas break, Nigel Godrich – who, since *OK Computer*, had worked with Beck, R.E.M. and Natalie Imbruglia - implemented a plan to speed the sessions along. The five members were split into two groups, neither of which could communicate with the other, nor pick up a rock instrument. After much programming, and swapping of discs crammed with interesting loops and samples, there was little real progress and the initiative was curtailed. In time, though, some things began to fall in place, and several tracks were regarded as 'in the bag' and given definitive titles. 'The National Anthem' was the track generally regarded as turning the sessions round, with 'In Limbo', 'Morning Bell' and 'Everything In Its Right Place' following soon after.

That spring, it was announced that the band had completed work on 24 titles, prompting rumours that the set would be a double album – an idea that Phil Selway was particularly vocal in dismissing as "unpalatable". By June 2000, a single album – now titled *Kid A* – was ready for mastering. And on a brief tour of Europe that summer, up to a dozen new songs, including 'Morning Bell', 'Optimistic' and 'The National Anthem', were premiered.

Radical enough for the band to consider releasing it under a pseudonym, difficult enough to split the members down the middle, *Kid A* is the pivotal album in Radiohead's career thus far. It quite deliberately dared to be different, and by its very nature, was destined to provoke. Most remarkable, though, was how receptive the wider audience was to this genuinely iconoclastic follow-up to *OK Computer*, which was soon installed at the top of the charts on both sides of the Atlantic.

"It was necessary to go away and glue back the pieces," said Thom Yorke. "In order to survive we had to stop being answerable." *Rolling Stone* magazine put it more dramatically: "To save themselves, Radiohead had to destroy rock'n'roll." Though no one quite said it at the time, *Kid A* – less a statesmanlike collection of rock songs than a 'But is it art?' gallery of sound – sounded just like a record for the 21st century. And there's been nothing like it since.

EVERYTHING IN ITS RIGHT PLACE

THOM YORKE'S catatonic moment backstage at the Birmingham NEC late in 1997 clearly disturbed him. Being rich, famous, successful and admired for his considerable creative gifts had done little to still his restless soul. "I was bored with saying I'd had enough. I was beyond that," he confessed to *Rolling Stone*. His head hot with confusion, his hands bored with his guitar, Yorke decided to buy a baby grand piano that he could barely play. He part-based his decision on an old Tom Waits quote he'd once read, that "what keeps him going as a songwriter is his complete ignorance of the instruments he's using". Perhaps a wild embrace with simplicity, naivety and 'the moment' would put 'everything in its right place'. It was a good maxim for the next couple of years, even if the theory was far easier to grasp than the practice. But in providing Yorke with a new method-

ology, the track was an obvious scene-setter for the album.

In contrast to the abrasive, percussion-heavy opening cuts on the previous two albums, 'Everything In Its Right Place' was a veritable chocolate box lid, its Carpenters-style electric piano intro soon joined by a gently repetitive Yorke vocal. Though the song's weird serenity was never fully demolished over the course of its four minutes, the 'right place' for Yorke – in actuality, his recorded voice manipulated into bite-sized chunks, then varispeeded, repeated and overlaid – seemed to be skimming at random across the deceptively liquid groove. If this was the sound of karmic correctness, then it was the Zen of the Korg Kaoss Pad (with which Greenwood manipulated Yorke's voice) that prevailed.

Incidentally, the singer's "sucking a lemon" reference is a pop at his former self, inspired he said, by the bitter, sunken-cheeked expression he'd been wearing the previous three years.

KID A

THERE is a Toytown ethnicity about this that brings to mind the quieter moments of This Heat, criminally neglected loop gurus from the late Seventies. But this is supposed to be the world's biggest band, capable of filling stadiums and shifting millions of units, not avant-rockers loved by John Peel and a small handful of his most daring listeners. Little wonder that The Wire magazine felt justified in putting Radiohead on its cover...

It's exactly this kind of computer-prompted piece that would have given the rest of the band sleepless nights, for 'Kid A' sounds like the work of a lone wolf with a gift for programming. And one who mistrusted the sound of his own voice, too, on the basis of the Vocoderised vocal that cuts through the piece as if the Fitter Happier 'voice' had returned out of its head on Owsley-strength California Sunshine. In fact, that wasn't too far from the truth. "I couldn't stand the sound of me anymore," Yorke later admitted. He also claimed that he would have felt uncomfortable singing the (undecipherable) lyrics, which can be found on a second sleeve, tucked away under the CD tray. "Absolutely brutal and horrible," the singer reckoned, though in truth, the randomly plucked lines look no more sinister in cold print than they sound on the record.

Incidentally, Phil Selway may have managed a 'real' drum part on this track, but two 'songs' in and Kid A was already defying all known rock conventions.

THE NATIONAL ANTHEM

THE opening notes of this, the most upbeat track on the album, served to remind listeners that this was, after all, a record by a recognised rock band, and not the latest addition to the Warp Records roster. But instead of heralding the expected crunch of guitar noise, the mesmerising intro bassline (played by Yorke some insist) just motors on alone in the manner of a metronomic Stereolab or Fall beat. In fact, where there was once a rock band, there's an eight-piece horn section, which eventually shatters the trance-like spell in honking, cacophonous fashion. Scored by Jonny Greenwood, who conducted the musicians with Thom utilising the little known method of hand-waving and leaping around, the big brass sound was intended to invoke the spirit of jazz giant Charlie Mingus. However, the effect was closer to mid-period Mothers Of Invention, or Captain Beefheart's similarly atonal 'Flash Gordon's Ape'.

Deemed important enough to open the set on the band's No Logo tour in summer 2000, timed to coincide with the album's release, 'The National Anthem' marked another turning point in the Kid A sessions. Having lost all confidence as a lyricist after OK Computer, Yorke declared his writer's block over after writing the four lines that largely constitute the words for this song.

Despite the singer's determination to break with the past, the key line, "Everyone has got the fear", reacquaints him with the paranoia-driven mood of the previous album. Oddly, it also brings another Charles Manson reference into the picture, for "getting the fear" was one of The Manson Family's psychological games in their war against the straight world.

HOW TO DISAPPEAR COMPLETELY

"IT SOUNDS like old Radiohead," Yorke once insisted, which is not surprising considering that it's one of the oldest tracks on the record. Written in the aftermath of his spiritual awakening at the Dublin show in mid-1997, there is a clear correlation between this and '(Nice Dream)' from *The Bends*. No surprise there, given the song's inspiration. "I dreamt I was floating down the Liffey (the river that flows through Dublin) and there was nothing I could do... The whole song is my experience of floating," Yorke claimed. He also admitted that one of the key phrases came to him during a telephone conversation with R.E.M.'s Michael Stipe. "I said, 'I cannot cope with this.' And he said, 'Pull the shutters down and keep saying, "I'm not here, this is not happening".'"

The title itself comes from a 1986 guide to identity change written by Doug Richmond, a theme that runs through the song – and, in many ways, throughout the album. Yorke's spellbinding opening, "That there, that's not me," sung over an acoustic backing that evokes Bowie's escapist classic, 'Space Oddity', is as succinct an instance of alienation as he'll ever write. Jonny Greenwood's contribution is crucial too, his string arrangement, indebted to Penderecki, lends the song a perfectly ghostly atmosphere.

TREEFINGERS

ON THE face of it a moody exercise in knob twiddling, this is actually a showcase for the hitherto under-utilised fretboard skills of Ed O'Brien, though you'd hardly know it. That's because Thom Yorke took a ten-minute blast of O'Brien feedback and other fretboard delights and twisted it out of all recognition into something akin to a lunar soundscape written for Kubrick's *2001: A Space Odyssey*. When the piece was used for the soundtrack of the 2000 film, *Memento*, the producers found an additional minute or so of music not heard on the album version.

Thom Yorke's insistence that "electronic music takes the emphasis off personalities" is no better illustrated than on this track, the first genuine instrumental in the band's album catalogue, and the piece that best suits the celestial mountain landscape of the cover artwork.

OPTIMISTIC

THOUGH deliberately coy about his lyrics during the making of the album, Yorke delivers this, the most wordy and overtly political song on the record, straight. Kid A's only recognisably 'Radiohead' track, 'Optimistic' (dig the irony) was recorded live in the studio, and features three drone-rock guitars and a Led Zep-style rhythm track. A brief return to rock, this track was sometimes referred to by insiders as 'Poptimistic', such was its relative proximity to normality.

Despite its brooding, hard rock beat, the closing "dinosaurs roaming the earth" mantra refers less to Page, Plant and friends than to the old network of politicians, military men and corporate leaders whose decisions continue to shape our daily lives. Naomi Klein's *No Logo*, a brilliant analysis of how the multinational ogres trample the globe like modern-day T-Rex's, informed much of Yorke's thinking at the time, and at one stage the title of her book was considered as a possible title for the album.

The hopeful "Try the best you can" quip was apparently supplied by Yorke's partner, Rachel, though the song's several animal references – which somehow conflate George Orwell and George Harrison's murderous 'Piggies' - bear all the twisted trademarks of a Yorke original.

Thanks to its big rock sound, 'Optimistic' was the first choice of alternative rock radio DJs across America.

IN LIMBO

PROBABLY the most provocative and distinguished track on the album, 'In Limbo' was also the shortest, clocking in at just over three-and-a-half minutes. Yorke once claimed the song reminded him of The Police, and though the association isn't a particularly pleasing one, you can hear what he means. It's all in the subtly flanged guitar arpeggios that skim hypnotically across the song's unquiet surface. The guitar isn't alone in creating what Yorke has called the song's "disorientating, floaty feel (that) comes from this really peculiar place". Yorke leads off with some Fender Rhodes playing that has all the etheral qualities of Chick Corea's contributions to the classic live 1970 Miles Davis line-up. And when that is faded out, a second guitar weaves its way around the gorgeously elusive rhythm, making a more than passable impression of Robert Fripp's work on those mid-Seventies Eno albums.

The song's original title, 'Lost At Sea', was even more appropriate than 'In Limbo', for its elusive qualities mirror perfectly the troubles Radiohead endured as they noodled and argued in Paris at the outset of the *Kid A* sessions. But it was dropped, probably because of its thematic proximity to Blur's 'This Is A Low' (both songs reference Radio 4's nightly shipping forecast, with Radiohead's boldly beginning with a direct quote: "Lundy, Fastnet and Irish Sea"). However, the key line in a song that evokes night-time cityscapes as much as it does lighthouses and bearded sea-dogs, is "I've lost my way", and it's one that still resonates magnificently.

IDIOTEQUE

WHILE much was made of Thom Yorke's blanket purchase of the entire Warp Records catalogue, this avant-dance track is the only piece on *Kid A* that owes a genuine debt to the fractured beats of the electronica specialists. Ironically, the only people other than the band to have earned money from the track were Paul Lansky and Arthur Krieger, two obscure electronic musicians from the Seventies. Samples from their contributions ('Mild Und Liese' and 'Short Piece' respectively) on an obscure album from 1976, *First Recordings – Electronic Music Winners*, were voluntarily acknowledged by the band. The track's air of urgent desperation is all Yorke's, though, his "We're not scaremongering/This is really happening" and "Ice Age coming" rants carrying all the ominous signs of *Blair Witch Project*-style terror. The solemn eruptions of keyboard chords also carry echoes of the Seventies; Kingdom Come's pioneering electro drum-machine *Journey* album in particular.

MORNING BELL

AS THE previous track fades into disarray, Yorke's distinctive Fender Rhodes electric piano intro-

duces one of the most popular songs on the album, a spacious production reminiscent of Public Image Ltd's magnificent *Metal Box*. The spritely, jazz-tinged rhythm belies the song's inner disturbance, which had been prompted by a trio of unfortunate mishaps. First, Yorke received a letter that lamented the fact that Thom Yorke was still alive while Jeff Buckley was dead. Then the singer claimed he experienced a visitation from a ghost in his south coast retreat. Finally, having sketched out the song on MiniDisc, a lightning storm promptly erased it. Some five months after losing it, Yorke was drifting off to sleep on a long-haul plane journey when it all came flooding back to him.

Little surprise, then, that he subsequently described the track – which boasted lyrics that seemed to be plucked right out of a street corner conversation - as "very, very violent. Extremely violent". While everyone around him appeared to be debating the pros and cons of Yorke's turn to 'laptop rock', the singer himself was apparently going through what he called "an unhealthy obsession with death". However, only this song, with its references to bumps on the head and cutting the kids in half, seem to dramatise his morbid thoughts in anything approaching a graphic manner. And given that 'Morning Bell' appears to concern itself with the aftermath of a relationship breakdown, the reference to sliced-up kids sounds disarmingly like black humour.

MOTION PICTURE SOUNDTRACK

UNLESS Thom Yorke was joking, this is the oldest track on the album. Apparently written around the time of 'Creep', 'Motion Picture Soundtrack' was readied for *OK Computer* but not used, then performed on several occasions during the 1997/'98 tours. By then, the song had three verses though – always performed by Thom Yorke on acoustic guitar – very little in terms of arrangement. Worked up again during the *Kid A* sessions, the track began to grow wings. And how...

When 'Motion Picture Soundtrack' opens, it sounds more solemn than ever, with a barely awake Yorke drawling his words as he pumps out the chords on a wheezy old harmonium. But at just over one and a half minutes, it's as if the heavens have opened and the forest has come alive. Jonny Greenwood teases out 'angel voices' on his Ondes Martenot, sampled harps conjure up lyre-plucking sirens at the Pearly Gates, and you'd be forgiven that this was some bizarre remake of The Beatles' 'Goodnight', which closes the 'White Album'. Though Yorke, who stumbles though the Disney-like scenario, complaining that "It's not like the movies/They fed us on little white lies", is hardly in the mood for Ringo Starr.

After Yorke's "I will see you in the next life" farewell, the song fades and there is exactly a minute's silence before the joyful angels and sirens return, only to disappear completely as the 'song' closes with the sound of another two minutes' silence. Radiohead had smuggled the musical teachings of John Cage to the top of the charts. Where to next?

Amnesiac

(Parlophone 7243 5 32764 2 3, April 2001)

THE BENDS, OK COMPUTER AND KID A HAD EACH BEEN, TO A LESSER OR greater extent, surprise packages; each either a significant advance on its predecessor or, in the case of *Kid A*, less an advance than an audacious defenestration of everything they'd achieved thus far. The most astonishing thing about *Amnesiac*, the band's fifth and perhaps most overlooked studio album, is that the surprise was that there was no surprise. Recorded during the same protracted batch of sessions as *Kid A*, and issued just six months afterwards, *Amnesiac* (or 'Kid B' as it's sometimes cheekily called) was hyped up prior to its release as "the Kid A that rocks". Though by no means entirely true, anyone wishing for the missing link between *Kid A* and *OK Computer* would not have been too disappointed.

When asked to compare *Amnesiac* with its predecessor, Colin Greenwood reckoned it was a record of extremes, one that mixed "more conventional" songs with "more dissonant" material. "*Kid A* is like a message recorded on your answerphone," he insisted. "*Amnesiac* is a good, direct conversation with someone." Thom Yorke was less secure in his assessment, responding to Nick Kent's "Are you happy with this record?" with a shoulder shrugging "I don't know". Almost two years had passed since the bulk of the album had been worked up, and – appropriately, given its title – *Amnesiac* was already suffering an identity crisis. Less dramatic than the jaw-dropping *Kid A*, the album was both conciliatory and a consolidation.

All fears that *Kid A* would sink the band had gone unrealised. With little overt publicity, no singles (or B-sides), no videos and only a handful of live dates, this record, which boasted few discernible hooks, and offered very little in the way of rock guitars or regular rhythms, topped the charts on both sides of the Atlantic. It was a huge triumph, shocking even, eclipsing even the achievements of *OK Computer* that, despite its dissonant edges, nevertheless included its fair share of raised arm singalongs.

Amnesiac couldn't hope to hold the attention the way *Kid A* had done. Its musical flavours were indeed more recognisably 'Radiohead'-like. And its release signalled the band's return as an active working unit. This time, there were the obligatory singles, promo videos and sell-out world tour, supported by a media blitz that had been deliberately absent for *Kid A*. Number 1 chart placings at home and in America too, confirmed the band as the most talked-about act on the planet. But still *Amnesiac* somehow lacked the sense of occasion that one had come to associate with each Radiohead release.

Any suspicion that the album consisted of leftovers from the *Kid A* sessions was instantly swept aside by a stunning three-song opening that boasted material at least as impressive as anything on *Kid A*. One, 'Pyramid Song', was instantly regarded as among the finest songs Radiohead had ever done. The material on *Kid A* had not been cherry-picked according to quality. It was simply a case of selecting "the best combination" of material, insisted Colin Greenwood. The crucial factor in the selection and sequencing of *Kid A* had been Thom Yorke's obsessive aversion to "so-called commercial melodies" ("like being besieged by a wasp," he groaned; "you just want it to go away"). That's why a lot of the more 'song' orientated material ended up on *Amnesiac*.

After the heady, palette-cleansing thrills of putting *Kid A* together, compiling a second set from the protracted *Kid A/Amnesiac* sessions proved more difficult. The material left at his disposal might have been at least as strong, at least on a track-by-track basis. But sculpting it into a coherent package – even allowing for Yorke's avowed "obsession with looking for accidents" – was no easier than all that handshaking on tour. Locking himself away for much of the autumn 2000 No Logo tour, Yorke eventually sequenced the record in time to meet the hoped-for spring 2001 release date.

Amnesiac belied its title, proving that even during their wilfully difficult late Nineties, Radiohead never fully jettisoned the rock band style they'd been patenting ever since *Pablo Honey*. Indeed, had they wished to present themselves in an evolutionary light, then *Amnesiac* and not *Kid A* would have been the rightful heir to *OK Computer*. Played in that context, the band's self-styled 'secret album' begins to sound like a classic record. Yep. Another one.

PACKT LIKE SARDINES IN A CRUSHD TIN BOX

As THE Eighties came into view, bands such as Throbbing Gristle, 23 Skidoo and Cabaret Voltaire headed an Industrial Music subculture that appeared to be on the cusp of a remarkable breakthrough. Taking punk's anti-rock rhetoric at face value, these genuine iconoclasts were intent on destroying the old rock'n'roll war-horse that had been in service for nigh-on 30 years. Adopting the guise of cultural terrorists, they eschewed guitars for electronic beats, songs for spoken-word 'samples', and were unafraid of drawing from a whole range of global influences (not to be confused with what's since become bastardised as happy-clappy 'world music'). This unprecedented development was sidelined when a new wave of guitar bands, including U2 and The Smiths (and R.E.M. in the States), heralded a new pop-rock revival, wiping out the more daring elements of the old independent sector. The more music biz-friendly 'indie' had arrived.

Much of what Radiohead achieved in the studio during 1999 and 2000 sounds like a continuation of the electronically charged post-punk adventure, refracted through the work of a range of contemporaries, from Aphex Twin to Underworld. The first bars of *Amnesiac* – a fractured electronic rhythm augmented by a kitchen utensil masquerading as an Eastern metallophone - also suggests that, far from being Radiohead's much-trumpeted 'return to rock', *Amnesiac* was more likely a toughened up *Kid A*.

Thom Yorke wrote the lyric while 'people watching' in the Place des Vosges in Paris, including the wonderfully tense and oft-repeated "I'm a reasonable man/Get off my case". One of the most memorable hooklines in (outré-)rock, this prompted a spontaneous mass singalong when Radiohead played the song at their homecoming Oxford show in July 2001.

PYRAMID SONG

WORDS can rarely ever do justice to something as abstract as musical sound. But in the case of 'Pyramid Song', it's tempting simply to direct the reader to the song without any further ado. A song of intense contrasts – a private piano piece that doubles as a vast, windswept epic, a unique fusion of classical, jazz, rock and the East –

'Pyramid Song' is a masterpiece of mesmerising sound and mystery-drenched imagery. It's still a pop record, but like 'Good Vibrations', 'Strawberry Fields Forever', and a small handful of truly transcendental singles, it's also a pocket-sized symphony that reveals new depths long after the novelty factor has worn off.

Although Yorke had bashed out a few preliminary chords on his new piano a few months earlier, the track truly took off in Copenhagen in March 1999 as a studio jam between Thom Yorke on piano, drummer Phil Selway and the spectre of a late, great jazz composer. "I was totally obsessed by a Charles Mingus song called 'Freedom'," Yorke later admitted, though equally prominent is the song's flamenco-like chord progression, which brings to mind the great West Coast psychedelic jams of the late Sixties. ('Spare Chaynge' on Jefferson Airplane's *After Bathing At Baxters* is the most obvious example.) With its swooping, mock-Eastern strings, stilted jazz rhythm, and Yorke's powerfully haunting vocal, 'Pyramid Song' is an incredibly sumptuous tapestry of delights that more than exceeded the sum of its influences.

'Pyramid Song' was premiered - as 'Nothing To Fear' - by Yorke and Jonny Greenwood in June 1999 at the Tibetan Freedom Concert in Amsterdam. A full band version was first unveiled, alongside several other new songs, at the Meltdown Festival at London's Festival Hall the following summer, by which time it had been retitled 'Egyptian Song'. Given the near triangular rhythm at its heart, 'Pyramid Song' seems an appropriate title, though Yorke has suggested there's a more rounded dimension to the piece, too.

Undermining his claim that the lyric took just five minutes to write, he then insisted that, like the music, it was pulled in "from all these mad places". Graham Hancock and Santha Falia's *Heaven's Mirror: Quest For The Lost Civilisation*, for example, which examined the links between ancient burial sites and astronomy. Stephen Hawking too, who "talks about the idea that time is completely cyclical. And that's something I've found in Buddhism, too. And that's what 'Pyramid Song' is about... that everything is going in circles... It's just this really beautiful thing that's just going round and round."

Chartwise, though, 'Pyramid Song' was more a simple case of up and down, entering at an impressive Number 5 before soon dropping out of sight. That doesn't make its achievement any less remarkable.

PULL/PULK REVOLVING DOORS

EVER the masters of queasy juxta-position, Radiohead chose to follow the scenic circularity of 'Pyramid Song' with the post-Industrial clutter of this exercise in sonic claustrophobia. All the endearingly human qualities of the previous track are harshly erased here, even Yorke's voice, fed through a studio Autotuner to give it that deadpan Genesis P-Orridge effect. (P-Orridge was frontman with Industrial Music pioneers Throbbing Gristle, whose work anticipated much of the Nineties 'difficult dance' explosion.)

The technological terror suggested by the abrasive beats is reflected in Yorke's 'fear of freedom' lyric which, though barely discernible, has a pronounced 'door' motif. This derived, he explained, from a scene in *Alice In Wonderland*, "where she walks down the corridor and there are lots of different doors. And I was in that corridor, mentally, for six months... Every door I opened, [I] was like, dreading opening it, 'cos I didn't know what was gonna happen next."

YOU AND WHOSE ARMY?

AND WHAT next after a vaguely apocalyptic piece invoking future dread and the tyranny of choice? Why, a song about political betrayal, of course. "Politics," Yorke admitted to *Mojo*'s Nick Kent, "was quite a big issue when we were doing this record." Or at least disillusionment with politics, which seems to have been the net effect of the first period of Tony Blair's 'New Labour' administration, which roughly coincided with the period between *OK Computer* and the *Kid A/Amnesiac* project. 'You And Whose Army?' is "ultimately about someone who is elected into power by people, and who then blatantly betrays them, just like Blair did," said the surprisingly plain-speaking Yorke.

His weary, Ink Spots-inspired vocal, set against some slothful blue-moon strumming, gives a disarming tone of resignation to what's actually a pub brawl of a lyric. And Yorke cracks a bit of a joke, too, the song's key refrain, "Come on if you think you can take us on", clearly inspired by a catchphrase associated with Phony Tony's most visible pop allies, Oasis ("Come on if you think you're hard enough"). Otherwise, there is little respite from the song's despairing tone. The arrival of the rest of the band two minutes into the song only provokes Yorke to scale new heights of whininess.

While (possibly too) much has been made of Radiohead's apparent tendency to wallow in misery, things don't get more grim than this. But then the subject matter is hardly the perfect scenario for a bit of upturned-thumb cheeriness, Paul McCartney style. Mercifully, at 3:11, 'You And Whose Army?' is the second shortest song on the album.

I MIGHT BE WRONG

HAVING rudely interrupted *Amnesiac*'s thrilling, initial three-song attack with their most unremittingly downbeat song yet, Radiohead seem in no hurry to clear the stale, oppressive air. In a different setting, the avant-punk intro riff of 'I Might Be Wrong' might have inspired thrilling comparisons with The Fall or even Beefheart's Magic Band. But here, despite being propped up by a deceptively uptight bassline, you'll struggle in vain to find even a hint of the characteristic elegance that usually softens the sorrow of the band's more difficult material. If 'I Might Be Wrong' was intended to give a bit of 'rock band' relief, it most certainly got it wrong. However, there is one moment of respite towards the end when, having reached some kind of groove-filled climax, the band pull away to reveal a spookily over-amped guitar lazily picking at the song's chords.

'I Might Be Wrong' was inspired by a vision that came to Yorke while looking back at his house during a walk along the nearby beach. Returning home to find nobody in the building, he sketched out the basis for the song, "with this presence still there".

This song was later used for the soundtrack of the Tom Cruise film, *Vanilla Sky*.

KNIVES OUT

THE mournful elegance that appeared to be the missing ingredient on the previous track returns with a vengeance on this, a near archetypal Radiohead song, and an instant fans' favourite. 'Knives Out' might sound like a breeze, its waterfall-like guitar lines echoing those of, say, 'Street Spirit' or 'No Surprises', but the track took a rumoured 313 hours to complete – despite getting the basics down at the start of the Copenhagen sessions. "It took 373 days to be arse-about-face enough to realise it was alright the way it was," sniffed Thom Yorke afterwards. No surprise, then, to discover that the song was hardly a favourite of his. The song's central theme was cannibalism which, given that Radiohead had virtually cannibalised their own work for the song, was rather apt.

AMNESIAC/MORNING BELL

ASKED why they had put out a second version of the penultimate track on *Kid A*, Thom Yorke explained: "It sounds like a recurring dream; it felt right."

The *Amnesiac* version of 'Morning Bell' is considerably less charm-filled than its more effervescent predecessor, complete with its bubbling rhythm track and more open sound. That doesn't make the song's presence here in any way bogus, for the slowed-down treatment introduces a distinctively sinister element to the song, enhanced further by a fairground element that is positively Hitchcockian. This radically reworked version also brings out the darker elements in Yorke's scattershot lyrics, those "Bump on the head" and "Cut the kids in half" references now sounding more like directions for a television drama series. Thom Yorke thought so too. "Sounds like *Tales Of The Unexpected*," he quipped.

DOLLARS AND CENTS

RADIOHEAD at their tense, nervous best. Initially, 'Dollars And Cents' showed little promise, at least according to Thom Yorke, who denounced the rhythm section's Can-type groove as "boring". Originally an 11-minute jam, laid down in Copenhagen in March 1999, the track was later trimmed back by over half for the finished version, a move that served to intensify its subtle dynamics. Also contributing to the song's trance-inducing quality is an Alice Coltrane sample, and an unsettling string arrangement by Jonny Greenwood. Continuing the Can theme, Thom Yorke's lyric – loosely concerned, as far as keen ears can tell, with the evils of the capitalist economy – is mumbled and whispered in the style of that band's legendary frontman, Damo Suzuki.

HUNTING BEARS

EVENING Bell' was the title Captain Beefheart once gave to one of the guitar instrumentals that were a regular feature of his records. If that had anything to do with 'Morning Bell', then it's never been publicly stated. But 'Hunting Bears', a Thom Yorke guitar piece (augmented by an unobtrusive computer-bass part), certainly bears some resemblance to those magical Magic Band interludes, even if it does start out like Thin Lizzy's 'Whisky In The Jar'. Further evidence that, despite its invigorating start, *Amnesiac* simply grows more down-beat as it goes on, 'Hunting Bears' at least provides a little exotic perfume to a record that - most uncharacteristically – threatens to descend into near ordinariness. *Mojo*'s David Cavanagh didn't quite see it that way. "A tuneless instrumental played on a slightly fucked-up guitar," he sniffed. He wasn't alone.

Incidentally, the song's title was inspired, Yorke once claimed, by a children's song, 'We're Going On A Bear Hunt', presumably a US equivalent to our own similarly bloodthirsty 'Run Rabbit Run'.

LIKE SPINNING PLATES

IF 'HUNTING BEARS' is the advance guard, then 'Like Spinning Plates' is the real thing, a truly hypnotising piece built around what sounds like an old analogue synthesizer wobble. Unsettling in the manner of a psychologically-charged Polanski movie, something that the imagery in the title manages to intensify, 'Like Spinning Plates' performs a wonderful balancing act between the avant-garde and soporific-inducing qualities of easy listening music. Little wonder that the song was once hailed by Thom Yorke as the best track on the record. 'Pyramid Song' excepted, it's certainly the freshest sounding.

The piece derived from part of another song, 'I Will'. In the studio, 'I Will' was playing backwards when Yorke realised that it actually sounded better that way. Suitably inspired, he then decided to write out a new batch of words based on the reverse vocals he'd heard, and then sung them forwards. Not that you'd know it, at least until the

words of the title emerge out of the sonic jungle, like some wonderful catharsis. It was, he admitted, "the most skew-whiff way of writing a song you could possibly imagine". And it worked.

LIFE IN A GLASSHOUSE

DESPITE all the wobbles and waywardness that preceded it, this closing song remains one of the more bizarre songs in the Radiohead canon. A neat subversion of the Dixieland jazz funeral lament, overlaid with all the tragedy of a Billie Holiday ballad, 'Life In A Glasshouse' also became the album's major talking-point, thanks to the appearance of 79-year-old jazz trumpeter Humphrey Lyttelton. That tended to overshadow what stands as one of Thom Yorke's finest lyrics, ostensibly inspired by the intrusive nature of the press but actually a neat summation of so many of his preoccupations.

The idea came to him after reading an article with a wife of a famous actor "who the tabloids completely hounded for three months like dogs from hell" he told Nick Kent. "She got the copies of the papers with her picture and pasted them up all over the house, over all the windows so that the cameras outside on her lawn only had their own images to photograph. I thought that was brilliant... From there it developed into a complete rant about tabloid journalism destroying people at will, tying people to the stake and watching them burn." Listen carefully and you'll also hear references to social iniquity and animal rights, the seemingly unquenchable thirst for a scapegoat and, as the closing "There's someone listening in" confirms, that old adversary, paranoia.

Wetter, happier: Radiohead's response to the enormous success of *OK Computer* was to dismantle their rock sound and embrace computer technology. The architect of that thrilling move was Thom Yorke, pictured here in 2000. *(Derek Ridgers/LFI)*

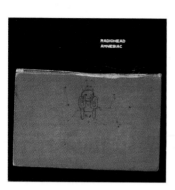

Amnesiac (2001).

Jonny Greenwood abandons his guitar for an old analogue keyboard during at the band's homecoming concert in Oxford's South Park, on July 7, 2001. It was Radiohead's only UK concert that year. *(Basil Clunes/LFI)*

Stubble man: Thom Yorke at South Park. For the first time in years, the band performed 'Creep', the final encore on a rain-spattered night. *(Basil Clunes/LFI)*

Radiohead's oft-overlooked trio, Colin Greenwood, Ed O'Brien and Phil Selway, flaunt a hat-trick of Grammys in Los Angeles, February 21, 2001. Kid A topped the Best Alternative Music Album category. *(Reuters/Corbis)*

From left, Thom Yorke performs with Ryan Adams, James Taylor and Neil Young at the latter's annual Bridge School Benefit concert, Shoreline Theatre, Mountain View, USA, on October 26, 2002. Earlier that evening, Yorke had ended his solo set with a version of Young's 'After The Goldrush'. *(Ilpo Musto/LFI)*

Another day, another accolade. Ed O'Brien and Colin Greenwood pose
with their distinctive Brat Award at *NME*'s annual awards ceremony,
London, February 25, 2002. *(David Fisher/LFI)*

Fears that Radiohead had sold their soul to Silicone Valley's corporate devil proved unfounded as they returned to guitars with a vengeance for 1993's *Hail To The Thief*. Thom Yorke and Colin Greenwood rock out at the Hollywood Bowl, California, September 26, 2003. *(George Campos/LFI)*

Although he hadn't completely abandoned his Ondes Martenot, Jonny Greenwood was back on his feet again for the 2003 tour. This shot was also taken at the acclaimed second night at the Hollywood Bowl. *(George Campos/LFI)*

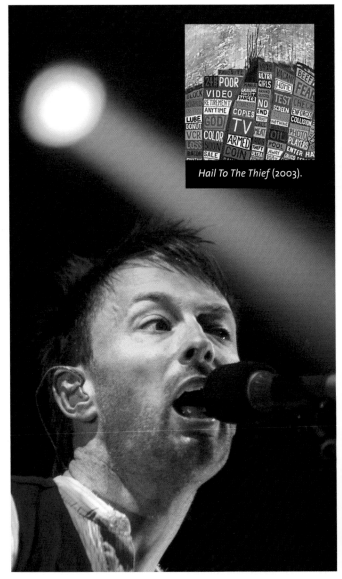

Hail To The Thief (2003).

Hail to the chief: Thom Yorke on stage in Brussels, Belgium, November 11, 2003. *(Gie Knaeps/LFI)*

Lost in music: Thom Yorke at the Coachella Music Festival, California, May 1, 2004. *(George Campos/LFI)*

Johnny Greenwood, Colin Greenwood and Phil Selway clutch their prestigious Ivor Novellos, awarded for International Achievement in songwriting, London, May 27, 2004. *(David Fisher/LFI)*

"We're basically old gits now," says Thom Yorke. But there are few signs that Radiohead are poised to surrender to the complacency that tends to blight rock bands once they hit middle-age. *(Martin Philbey/Redferns)*

I Might Be Wrong: Live Recordings

(Parlophone 7243 5 36616 2 5, November 2001)

TRACKS: The National Anthem/I Might Be Wrong/Morning Bell/Like Spinning Plates/Idioteque/Everything In Its Right Place/Dollars And Cents/True Love Waits

IF *PABLO HONEY* **IS THE RUNT OF THE RADIOHEAD LITTER, THEN THIS, THE MOST** invisible of the band's albums, is more akin to a phantom pregnancy. Issued hot on the heels of *Kid A* and *Amnesiac* – and three albums in 13 months was certainly going some - *I Might Be Wrong* has the distinction of being the least eagerly awaited Radiohead record. Essentially, a collection of mildly diverting concert versions of familiar material, it is also the most superfluous. So much so that even its makers seemed content to let it out with little fanfare, slipping it into the schedules with the minimum of promotional hoopla, and slapping on a mid-price tag that instantly devalued the product.

Live albums are often rotten affairs, though that's not always been the case. During the psychedelic late Sixties, for example, bands such as The Grateful Dead and The Pink Floyd regarded live performance as the true theatre of creative endeavour. Studio recordings were strictly secondary affairs, diversions from the 'real thing', and both acts could hardly wait to release labyrinthine live albums. In the punk era, too, when producers struggled to capture the energy of the new wave bands in a studio, live recordings played an important role. But more often than not, rock and pop concerts are little more than happy-clappy affairs punctuated by identikit – and invariably weaker - versions of an artist's greatest hits, artlessly delivered yet rapturously received.

I Might Be Wrong is hardly *Live Dead* or *Ummagumma*, or *Live At The Roxy* for that matter, but neither is the proverbial purse-snatcher. For a start, there are no hits. *The Bends* and *OK Computer*, still the band's most highly regarded albums, are not represented at all. And, of course, there's not a hint of 'Creep'. Instead, with the exception of the song that closes the set, the material on *I Might Be Wrong* is drawn exclusively from *Kid A* and *Amnesiac*. Churlish? A little, perhaps. But with both records commonly regarded as painstakingly assembled studio creations, a triumph of computer technology over human endeavour, *I Might Be Wrong* was proof that the material could work equally well in the live context. And instead of being faced by machines, the audience saw it performed by an all too human five-piece rock band. The all too audible party-like atmosphere confirmed that this was not merely music for chin-strokers.

"Everyone is so near," wails Thom Yorke on the opening 'The National Anthem', and you feel for him. You might be wrong, of course. The group's reputation for interminably long studio sessions, not to mention their tendency to eschew the rock'n'roll lifestyle for the comforts of home, has tended to erase the fact that it was through a hectic gigging schedule that Radiohead secured their reputation. Even during the difficult days, when weeks of seemingly fruitless studio endeavour would turn into months, the band tended to clear the air by going out on the road. And, interspersed between the arm-waving anthems, would be a sizeable chunk of new material.

But unveiling new work wasn't the point of *I Might Be Wrong* which, if not exactly a contract-fulfilling release, certainly had something of the obligatory 'tour souvenir' about it. Even though a handful of new songs were regularly performed on the spring/summer 2001 *Amnesiac* tour, none made it onto this record. The only 'new' song, in fact, was 'True Love Waits', a fans' favourite that had first been introduced into the live set in December 1995. *I Might Be Wrong*, which didn't exactly prompt a stampede when it appeared in November 2001 – scraping into the Top 30 in the UK and the Hot 50 in the States – was more a case of... But I Think I'm Right, tangible proof that Radiohead's 'difficult' material wasn't quite so alienating after all.

After a brief dial-twist of world band radio noise, 'The National Anthem' kicks in, introducing the idea that Radiohead are in fact some kind of trance-rock band. If John Lydon had formed PiL with ex members of Gong, instead of his mates from Bash Street, they might have sounded like this. Neither as freak-funky as early Seventies Miles Davis, nor as lysergically entrancing as Can (both acts at least as influential in the Nineties as they were in their own time), 'The National Anthem', here even more reliant on its simple, overfuzzed bass riff, sounds tough and rudimentary.

And that's pretty much the story of this stopgap album: stripping back much of the material's more fanciful flourishes and ProTools-inspired trickery, the songs' artful structures now carry the day. But things don't always work out as one would imagine.'I Might Be Wrong', one of the more recognisably 'rock' tracks on the set, actually sounds perfunctory here. Yet from its opening digital drum beat to its anti-climactic finale, 'Morning Bell', the track that follows it, is rapturously received. Stranger still, 'Like Spinning Plates', one of the more unlikely cuts from the *Kid A/Amnesiac* sessions to be taken out on the road, has been reworked to stunning effect. In fact, so complete is the transformation – a necessity due to the reverse-technology nature of the original - that it's almost a minute before a wave of recognition hits the crowd. 'Like Spinning Plates' has become an intense and beautifully solemn piece of chamber music, and yet its lyric despair still works wonderfully on the international stage. Yorke's opening "While you make pretty speeches/You cut me to shreds" is so quietly powerful, and epitomises the song's drawing-room anger. All that is grotesquely magnified by the audience cheers, which provide a bizarre contrast to the 'floating bodies' imagery that inevitably conjure up images from the appalling inter-tribal conflict witnessed in Rwanda during 1994.

The spectre of mass genocide also haunts the next track, 'Idioteque', its urgent warnings of "Ice Age coming!" and "This is really happening!" eclipsed by Yorke's barely controlled repetition of the phrase "Violence to the children" at the song's end. The strangest sound of all, though, again comes from the crowd, who appear to join Yorke – who has trimmed the lyrics for this live version – in a mass choral of "this is really happening!"

At well over seven minutes, 'Everything In Its Right Place' is the longest track on the record, and something of a relief after the album's descent into the heart of darkness. Once the first, extraordinary evidence that *Kid A* was not going to be *OK Computer* Vol. 2, its keen reception here shows how far Radiohead had taken their audience with them. It's a pity, then, that the performance here is overlong, and lacks the head-spinning ambience of the studio version. The crowd's enthusiastic, on-the-beat handclaps that greet its opening bars also tend to shatter the song's spellbinding effects.

The penultimate track, 'Dollars And Cents', also lacks the character of its studio counterpart, though that's forgotten almost as soon as the opening chords of 'True Love Waits' are struck. Heralding a most glorious finale, this is the performance that transforms *I Might Be Wrong* from a mildly diverting curio into a minor treasure-trove.

If Thom Yorke has ever affected desolation better than that moment, midway through 'True Love Waits', when he sings, "I'm not living/I'm just killing time", I've yet to hear it. Sung over a simple, though compelling acoustic guitar figure, this song is the closest Yorke has ever come to the spectacularly haunted work of Pink Floyd's psychedelic poet-prince Syd Barrett, and his 1969 outtake, 'Opel', in particular. A song of acute desperation, 'True Love Waits' brilliantly inverts the sentiments of the old Buddy Holly song, and it's a measure of the band's thirst for perfection that they've still only released the song in this solo acoustic live form. And it's not been for want of trying. 'True Love Waits' was namechecked more than once in Ed O'Brien's online diaries at the beginning of 2000. "It is a great song," he wrote, hinting that it might just find its way onto the new album (*Kid A*). "It's simply trying to find a way of doing it which excites us," he explained. It's a pity that space wasn't found for 'True Love Waits' on the

Hail To The Thief

(Parlophone 7243 5 84805 2 8, June 2003)

AFTER THAT CONTROVERSIAL DOUBLE-STRENGTH SWING TO THE LEFT, THE "swagger" back towards centre stage. At least, that was the message that seemed to emanate from the band's direction during the run-up to the release of the sixth Radiohead studio album. Not everyone saw it quite that way. Parallels with the uneven and sometimes uneasy soundclashes on *Amnesiac* were all too easily made. Even Thom Yorke seemed worryingly – and uncharacteristically – laid-back about the record and the band's changing role in the new rock order. "We've had our moment," he told *Q* magazine, only half in jest. "We're old! We had it and that's great. Now I'm tired of picking a fight... making grandiose statements. We've made an album and it's kinda there. No pressure. Nothing to live up to."

If that sounded like an admission of defeat, then much of the music on the record served to undermine his suspicions. (If anything, his comments might have encouraged the rather disproportionate number of armchair psychologists out there in Radioheadland to start fantasising about a Thom Yorke solo album.) So did the views of his fellow band members, all of whom seemed to have had a ball working on *Hail To The Thief*, especially after the 'pulling teeth' methodology employed during the making of the previous two studio sets. "I'll be honest. I don't like [*Amnesiac*] very much," Ed O'Brien told *Q*, adding that it had been "too cerebral". The difference this time, he said, was *swagger*. "We learned to swagger as a band," O'Brien added, referring to their 2001 American tour. "We wanted to capture that on record." And, this time, the band were keen to reacquaint themselves with the ancient rock'n'roll art of limiting songs to as close to three minutes as possible. The idea was to breeze in and out of the recording studio, not treat it as a second home. "Keeping it succinct," was the key, claimed O'Brien.

But anyone who imagined that the songs on the new Radiohead album would form an orderly queue, just like they had done on *The Bends* was bound to be disappointed. Perhaps expectations of a return of the 'classic', poll-topping Radiohead sound, had been raised too high. That was certainly the case in the mainstream music press, where tolerance for the band's deconstruction of rock'n'roll had been running out for some time. Sure, there was a greater sense of rock band unity on *Hail To The Thief*, as well as more drums, bass and guitars than on any Radiohead record since 1997. But the skills learned during the protracted *Kid A/Amnesiac* sessions had not been forgotten. In fact, at times it felt that now all five band members were fully committed to the art of tearing the structures apart.

If all the 'right' instruments were now back in the mix, that didn't necessarily mean the mix itself had to conform to any recognisable standard. And as for that old verse/chorus/verse organising structure... forget it.

There was, however, a unifying vibe about *Hail To The Thief* that was a clear consequence of the new 'methodology' (to use the correct Radiohead terminology) employed during its making. Around the time of *Kid A*, Thom Yorke admitted that the group operated "like the U.N.", with him playing the role of "America", the bully who'd wave a big stick until he got his way. Early in 2002, as the band began to think about 'the next project', Ed O'Brien, initially the most vocal opponent of the see-what-happens *Kid A* approach, proposed that it was time for a change. Thom Yorke would supply a disc's worth of demos by mid-spring. The band would spend the next three months working on the material, the best of which would then be included in the set during the summer tour. Then, at the end of the dates, the band would record the new album in one whirlwind, two-week session.

The plan worked – more or less. Things looked good when Yorke supplied not one but three CDRs, crammed full of demos sung solo to either a guitar or piano backing. Each disc was given a title – *The Gloaming*, *Episcoval* and *Hold Your Prize* – which, O'Brien later told *Q*, "he hadn't [done] for five years. It reminded me of tapes for *OK Computer*. This is the way it used to be. It signified that he was ready to engage again." Better still, Yorke's demos were composed with more consideration than usual. According to Colin Greenwood, "He was really careful to give us stuff that was as neutral and as bland as possible, so that we would be able to work together on providing music."

The band distilled the best of Yorke's ideas into one disc's worth of material, and unveiled the best of them in Lisbon on July 22. By the end of the tour a month later, the new material had really begun to 'gel', according to Ed O'Brien. "You know that time when bands begin to swagger, like when the Stones got in a groove from '68 to '73?," he said. "I think we've done that."

Eschewing wintry Paris or cold Copenhagen, where they'd laid down the basis for the previous two studio albums, Radiohead decamped to Los Angeles. Working in the smog-bound heart of the beast, at Ocean Way in West Hollywood to be exact, proved a liberating experience, somewhat ironic, given the record's subject matter. (It had been Nigel Godrich's suggestion to record in California, where he'd previously worked with Beck and Travis.)

Despite the band's initial reservations, sessions "were fun, they really were", Thom Yorke told *Q* magazine in 2003. When they weren't working, the band played at being tourists: driving out to the desert, roaming the metropolis in hired cars and feasting on the obligatory food mountains. But when in the studio, they more or less kept to their rule of recording one song per day, in 12-hour sessions that would last from midday to midnight.

In October 2002, after the band had spent an additional couple of weeks on the tapes at their Oxfordshire studio, Ed O'Brien insisted that all was "sounding good... a lot of energy. I always say it's gonna be an album of three-minute pop songs... but that's what it is this time," he said confidently. After final touches were added in January 2003, the finished album was ready to be mastered by early March. "To me, this record feels like the culmination of the best bits of *The Bends*, *OK Computer*, *Kid A* and *Amnesiac*," O'Brien reckoned, and before the month was out, eager fans were able to judge for themselves as an early mix of the record was made available on the internet. "Ain't that a bitch," said Godrich. "Stolen work," added Jonny Greenwood. "Wait until you see the final, real, finished album!" said the ever-cheerful Colin Greenwood. Thom Yorke was probably too angry to add his comments.

In July 2001, Radiohead had been the cover stars of that month's *Mojo* magazine. Elsewhere in that issue was an obituary of punk rock legend Joey Ramone. The piece was titled "Hail, Hail To The King". Whether that had helped prompt Yorke to drop the working title, *The Gloaming*, is not known. Certainly, the phrase *Hail To The Thief* was already in common currency by this time, used by doubters who inverted George Bush's Hail To The Chief slogan in the wake of his dubious victory in the 2000 US Presidential elections. The rest of the band had felt *The Gloaming* – which referred to those precious minutes of twilight before nightfall – sounded like a progressive rock title. And besides, Yorke's growing political sophistication, customary cynicism and thoughts as a new father (a son, Noah, was born to him and Rachel in February 2002), all pointed towards a more obviously dynamic album title.

In that *Mojo* article, Yorke had declared himself "chuffed to bits" about Bush's election, "because it's going to radicalise people". His optimism was rudely curtailed just a couple of months later, when the post-9/11 world revealed itself in the grip of an ugliness greater even than Thom Yorke had imagined. With America on the offensive as it sought to maintain (and extend) its hegemony in the new century, and the majority of its population backing Bush in his so-called "war against terror", it was no time to be seen to be upsetting the Land Of The Free. After all, if the much-respected Noam Chomsky, Susan Sontag and Naomi Klein were having a rough time of it, then what hope a whining boy from a country that didn't even believe in capital punishment?

"I don't see the title or the record as a political statement at all," Yorke backtracked, when the album appeared in June 2003. "I see politics, in terms of control of one's own life, being removed permanently anyway." He explained it a little differently to *Spin* magazine. "The trouble with your question [about the title] is that if I discuss the details of what I'm referring to... I will get death threats. And I'm frankly not willing to get death threats, because I value my life and my family's safety. That sort of sucks, I realise, but I know what is going on out there."

Indeed he does, perhaps a little too well for his own comfort. But however much the album was pointed at the outrageous behaviour that surely one day the history books will get right, it was true: no Radiohead album was simply just about One Big Idea, let alone One Peculiar President. "I was just overcome with all this fear and darkness," Yorke expanded. "And that fear is The Thief."

2+2=5 (THE LUKEWARM)

THE CD booklet reveals that the album's 'shadow' title is *The Gloaming*. Likewise, each song is given an alternate title in parenthesis. Taken literally (not always a good idea with Yorke's lyrics), this one's totally misleading, because there's nothing lukewarm about this arresting opener. The first sound we hear is Jonny Greenwood plugging his guitar into an amp, the first act of the first session. It prompts a "That's a nice way to start, Jonny" quip from Thom Yorke.

The song itself begins with a wonderfully succinct accusation ("Are you such a dreamer?/To put the world to rights?"), before the hypnotic guitar/drum interplay takes hold, undergoes several dramatic mutations – including a 'Savoy Truffle'-style George Harrison falsetto - before its punkish, manic finale.

Yorke subsequently claimed that '2+2=5' had been "totally" inspired by listening to news programmes on Radio 4. The meaning behind the song's key, repeated phrase, "You have not been paying attention", appears all too obvious. Although it's not quite true that no one listens to Radio 4 except for politicians and lecturers, Yorke is only too aware that 'real' news has been eclipsed by the audience's desire for 'infotainment'. His explanation of 'the Lukewarm', which he picked up from girlfriend Rachel, who once studied Dante's *The Inferno*, is helpful here. "The Lukewarm... didn't believe in anything particularly," he told XFM's John Kennedy. "They were like, 'Oh, you know, whatever, there's nothing I can do about it." After which, he cried, "No, no, no!!!!"

The reference, towards the end of the song, to "the king" and "the sky falling in" is taken from *Chicken Licken*, a popular infant-school tale that ends with a gratified fox licking its lips. "I love that idea of there being no intention of a happy ending," Yorke confessed.

SIT DOWN. STAND UP
(SNAKES & LADDERS)

HOPES that *Hail To The Thief* was the much fancied 'return to rock' it had been trumped up to be collapsed as soon as 'Sit Down. Stand Up' begins. A digital drum, an eerie synth and a dreamy xylophone, with Yorke's white sheet of a voice sanctimoniously imploring us to "walk into the jaws of hell" neither rocked nor rolled. Thom's toytown apocalypse was back, and so too was the technological frenzy that marked – some say blighted - the *Kid A/Amnesiac* sessions. And with a climax as manic and/or disturbed as this - Yorke huffs and puffs "The raindrops" no less than 46 times against a sonic backdrop that sounds more like an Aphex Twin backing track than rain – one can only imagine smiles of joy, and not puzzlement, on the faces of aficionadoes.

Written around the time of *OK Computer*, 'Sit Down. Stand Up' was apparently inspired by the Rwanda conflict. But Yorke's "We can wipe you out anytime" was, he explained, inspired by a new missile that is able to locate its target using only a signal from a mobile phone.

SAIL TO THE MOON
(BRUSH THE COBWEBS OUT
OF THE SKY)

BOTH Thom Yorke and Jonny Greenwood have described this tender, cautiously optimistic song as their favourite on the album. Written as a response to the birth of his son Noah – cue Biblical reference: "Or in the flood/You'll build an Ark/And sail us to the moon" – it was, said dad, "a hopeful song". And in namechecking *The Moonbeams*, Yorke was inspired to look back at his own childhood. According to Greenwood, 'Sail To The Moon' hadn't always sounded quite so charming. Initially "only half an idea" and not "very well-written", the guitarist said the song only came together after the rest of the band fleshed out Yorke's initial sketch. Even the sometimes reticent Phil Selway got embroiled in the arrangement, his intermittent, delicate drumming doing much to enhance the song's enchanting mood.

BACKDRIFTS
(HONEYMOON IS OVER)

THE BBC Radiophonic Workshop would have been proud of this, dominated by a wobbly synth that seems to be playing an ambient version of the theme from *Doctor Who*. Despite the song's seemingly melody- free backing, Yorke drags a decent tune out of it, one apparently inspired by a spectacular blanket of snow he'd chanced upon while in Japan.

Before starting work on the album, Yorke was insisting that the sessions would be free from the computer technology that drove the *Kid A/Amnesiac* sessions. The cold, cut-up sounds of 'Backdrifts' suggest his resolve wasn't as firm as he'd intended. Incidentally, the song's subtitle employs a phrase often thrown in the direction of the Blair administration, which had managed to dash so many hopes within so few months of taking office.

GO TO SLEEP
(LITTLE MAN BEING ERASED)

THERE'S a folkishness about this song – and especially Thom Yorke's vocal - that stretches all the way from the Olde Englishness of Fairport Convention to the soar-away bleats of California's Tim Buckley, recently back on the singer's playlist. Also back in the picture for the first time since being namechecked on 'Anyone Can Play Guitar' is Jim Morrison, pastiched when Yorke drawls out, "We don't want the loonies taking over", itself sounding like a line from the (Pink Floyd's) Roger Waters songbook. The song's folkish demeanour, complete with round-the-Maypole-style hop-a-long riff, breaks down midway through the song, when the guitars and drums interlock, and shift up a gear into a fabulous Krautrock-like groove.

WHERE I END AND YOU
BEGIN
(THE SKY IS FALLING IN)

THERE'S a distinct whiff of The Stone Roses about this unexceptional indie-dance song, especially the moodily echoed voice, and the insistent drum pattern, which had

been ripped from Can's Jaki Liebezeit anyway. Perhaps it was all a subtle tribute to 'Madchester', whose New Order also seemed to be the inspiration for the bassline. Toss in a melody that appears to prompt Thom Yorke into Bono mimickry, and we're looking at one of the most derivative songs in the Radiohead catalogue.

Ostensibly an examination of the alienation factor in otherwise close relationships, the lyrics occasionally stray into potentially political territory, the early reference to dinosaurs roaming the earth matched up with the closing, "And there'll be no more lies". "I really don't know what on earth these words mean," Yorke shrugged at the time of the album's release. Inevitably, a million fans and commentators thought they did.

WE SUCK YOUNG BLOOD
(YOUR TIME IS UP)

THIS dirge-like evocation of the pre-Nazi Weimar Republic, given additional twists of Nick Cave and Tom Waits, provides the obligatory lull that features at the centre of every Radiohead album – give or take that brief moment midway through the song when it tumbles into Tindersticks-style action. The hammy title is quite appropriate for a song that sinks its fangs into those vampiric latter-day celebrities who, having been vacuum-packed for public consumption, feed off younger talents in order to retain their status. Inevitably, there's a hint of self-reflection in the song –

"We're basically old gits now," Yorke admitted at the time – though the main target was clearly the film industry: "Hollywood and the constant desire to stay young, fleece people, suck their energy," Yorke explained. That probably wasn't enough to rescue Radiohead's interminable goth moment from the clutches of eternal sleep.

THE GLOAMING
(SOFTLY OPEN OUR MOUTHS
IN THE COLD)

FROM the ugly world of vampiric celebs to the alluring beauty of the English countryside at nightfall, otherwise known as 'The Gloaming'. What once looked destined to become the title track also picks up on the "sky is falling in" theme set out in '2+2=5', a terrible beauty that only magnifies the apocalyptic thinking that lies at the heart of so many Radiohead songs. So no surprises when Thom Yorke explained the song's meaning in the simplest of terms: "It's about the feeling I had that we're entering an age of intolerance and fear".

'The Gloaming' – "A very out of fashion word for twilight," Yorke told XFM listeners – harks right back to the darkest, staring-at-a-computer-screen days of the *Kid A* sessions, though for this song, Colin Greenwood was at Yorke's side to assist with the programming. Yorke, of course, needed no help coming up with lines such as, "Murderers, you're murderers/We are not the same as you".

'The Gloaming' "had this ominous nature that stuck with me," he told *Q* magazine. "It was all wrapped up with the fact that I found it incredibly difficult to come to terms with the fact that maybe we were leaving our children with no future at all."

THERE THERE
(THE BONEY KING OF
NOWHERE)

IF THERE'S a piece of music in rock's 50-year history that leaves the listener gasping for more as much as this does, when it fades after a measly five minutes and 23 seconds, I've yet to hear it. From its assured, massed tom-tom intro, 'There There' just builds and builds, exploding majestically at three minutes, and then again at four, before coming to a dignified conclusion. For once, an undignified extended version would have been fully justified; the fine art of rock at its trance-inducing best deserves all the space it can get. And it's no surprise at all to learn that Thom Yorke wept uncontrollably when he heard the first playback of the song, the basis of which was recorded live in the band's Oxfordshire studio. Radiohead will have trouble topping this, and maybe Yorke knew it.

Everything seems to be in its right place. The ceaseless, spellbinding voodoo beat; the rattle and hum of gently overamped electric guitars; and that extraordinary siren of a voice "singing you to shipwreck". A couple of minutes in and it gets even better, the song's vampish charms simply impossible to resist. The windswept melody turns into a tornado, the guitars glide and collide with cruel repetition, and you'd be forgiven for thinking this was some clue-sodden classic of Renaissance art come to life. OK: composure. After all, as the song itself has it: "Just cos you feel it doesn't mean it's there". Maybe so, but there's something about 'There There' that's up there, transcendentally meditating beside the best work of Miles Davis or Jimi Hendrix.

When asked about the song, Thom Yorke invoked a third party of innovators. It was, he said, partly a homage to Can, and specifically, their *Tago Mago* album. But besides classical antiquity and classic Krautrock, there was another, more direct influence. Failing to engage his son with a DVD's worth of vintage episodes of the Seventies children's television series, *Bagpuss*, Yorke decided to watch all 13 himself. Episode Two, The Owls Of Athens, struck a particular chord, especially a song called 'The Boney King Of Nowhere'. That gave 'There There' its secondary title, though its uncertain how much of Yorke's lyric derives from the tale, which concerned "a pipe-cleaner king with a bony arse who moans about the hardness and coldness of his throne", according to Yorke. The band approached the series' maker, Oliver Postgate, to create a video for the song – but Postgate declined the offer.

I WILL (NO MAN'S LAND)

FIRST glimpsed, albeit briefly, in the *Meeting People Is Easy* video, 'I Will' is, at just under two minutes, one of Radiohead's most concise recordings. First attempted during the *Kid A* sessions, that keyboard-enriched version eventually became the reverse electronics maelstrom that was 'Like Spinning Plates'. By the time it was reworked for *Hail To The Thief*, 'I Will' had different lyrics and spartan guitar-and-piano accompaniment.

A strangely delicate indictment of war, the song deals explicitly with one particularly ghastly episode from the first Gulf War, "when a missile hit that bunker which wasn't a weapons dump at all, it was full of women and children". Yorke later said it was "the angriest thing I've ever written".

A PUNCHUP AT A WEDDING (NO NO NO NO NO NO NO)

IT'S A black humoured man who chooses to sequence a song titled 'I Will' next to one that invokes a not untypical feature of the post-marriage piss-up. There's nothing particularly amusing, or distinguished, about the song, though, an early bird from the *Thief* sessions that swings soulfully to little real effect. Eager-eared acid-rockers no doubt spotted some similarities with Hawkwind's similarly groovy 'Time We Left This World Today'. "Baggy swagger," summed up Yorke.

MYXOMATOSIS (JUDGE, JURY & EXECUTIONER)

MUCH commented on at the time of the album's release, this isn't actually the first song to namecheck the virus that virtually wiped out Britain's rabbit population during the Fifties. (Marc Bolan got there first with 'Left Hand Luke' on T. Rex's *Tanx* album, issued in 1973.) "I loved the word," said Yorke, who could remember his parents discussing the episode at home. But, he added, his song was actually about mind control.

Driven by a demonic, fuzzed-up bass riff, 'Myxomatosis' had been the band's first choice to work on having digested Yorke's three CDRs worth of demos. "The nasty one," said the surprised songwriter. It's one of the wordiest songs on the album, too, evolving from a short story Yorke had written then cut up, in the style of another mind control freak, William Burroughs. If the chorus sounds familiar, that's because the words had been previously used for another similarly narcotic number, the 'Knives Out' B-side, 'Cuttooth'.

SCATTERBRAIN (AS DEAD AS LEAVES)

DURING the Great Storm of 1987, one man was actually killed by a beach hut that had been lifted from its foundations by the surprise hurricane. In the deceptively sedate 'Scatterbrain' another man battles "a force ten gale", a witness to the struggling birds and the ruined roofs, who may or may not meet a similarly sticky end thanks to another freak of nature ("Lightning fuse/powercut"). The spectre of the howling wind also summons up the 1939 film, *The Wizard Of Oz*, which boasts a famous house-raising incident, as well as a scatterbrained 'Scarecrow'. If *The Wizard Of Oz* is the song's inspiration, then 'Scatterbrain' hardly rates alongside Bowie's 'Life On Mars' (an acknowledged *Oz*-inspired tale), though it does boast one of Thom Yorke's prettiest melodies.

A WOLF AT THE DOOR (IT GIRL. RAG DOLL)

ANOTHER song that has its origins in the sessions for *Kid A/ Amnesiac*, 'A Wolf At The Door' is something of a Radiohead rarity. That's because the music was written entirely by Jonny Greenwood, with the notable exception of the Beethoven-derived 'Moonlight Sonata' motif that runs throughout, of course.

If not quite a swagger, this song certainly has a lovely, waltz-time lilt to it, which in turn inspires a wordy contribution from Yorke. Sounding remarkably like snatched dialogue from a particularly nightmarish evening in front of the telly, the lyrics actually derive from something more awful still, when Yorke was "having a complete nervous breakdown". The memorable "flan in the face" phrase refers to an incident in March 2001 when a pal of

EXTRA TRACKS

1. B-sides, Stray A-sides, Remixes, etc.

The *Pablo Honey* Era

STUPID CAR

THOM YORKE doesn't rate cars much. And not simply for worthy ecological reasons, either. Back in 1987, he was involved in a car accident, the likely catalyst for a theme that's littered throughout Radiohead's work. Needless to say, this sparse, early venture (a leftover from the On A Friday days), and the only one of the four songs on *The Drill* EP that wouldn't be re-recorded for inclusion on *Pablo Honey*, is hardly Yorke's definitive treatment on the subject.

INSIDE MY HEAD

YORKE begins this with a highly mannered, "What do you want from me?", which has all the hallmarks of a young man who's just been given a record deal and wants everyone to know about it. Fuelled by a classic combination of arrogance and insecurity, 'Inside My Head' includes a decidedly self-conscious reference to "that syringe", and a self-deprecating admission to possessing "the English disease". On the evidence of this, that probably means too much Gang Of Four on the turntable though in truth, the song has all the aplomb of a band who just want to become Oxford's answer to The Pixies. Co-producer Paul Kolderie, who'd worked with The Pixies, assumed that he'd been deliberately given a "weak" song to work with as a test to see what wonders he could cook up with his partner Sean Slade in the studio.

MILLION $ QUESTION

A REGULAR feature of the 1992 shows, this song blusters along with all the excitement and urgency of a band who've just signed their first proper record deal. In a sign of things to come, Yorke shares his misgivings about the entire venture, topping and tailing it by insisting he'd always been "waiting for the crush" at the start, then ending it with a vainglorious "I hope they miss me" directed at his ex-employers. 'Million $ Question' is tucked away on the flip of the original 'Creep' single, though it's hardly one of the better known B-sides, and for good reason.

FAITHLESS, THE WONDERBOY

MUSICALLY, this sounds remarkably like a reprise of 'Prove Yourself'. Lyrically, too, it seems to look backwards, all the way to Thom Yorke's childhood (and, just maybe, those episodes of *Champion, The Wonderhorse*). There's a strong suspicion that the sense of isolation in the song - "And all my friends say bye bye" – mirror Yorke's own. Forced to endure several operations on a lazy left eye, which was sometimes covered with an eye-patch, invariably marked him out as 'different'. The singer has always insisted that he wasn't "kicked around", though 'Salamander', as he was sometimes unkindly called, would inevitably have fantasised about a time when he could enjoy the peace that the "other boys" seemed to enjoy. Rather than any more obvious rock-'n'roll lifestyle connection, the song's repeated phrase, "Can't put the needle in", is more likely a reference to Yorke's own early brushes with remedies and medicines.

A B-side coupling with 'Anyone Can Play Guitar', 'Faithless, The Wonderboy' was a regular in the band's live sets during 1993.

COKE BABIES

PERHAPS the emerging Easy Listening revival had narked him? Thom Yorke uses the word 'Easy' no less than 14 times in this mildly impressive bridge between an FX-led shoegazing dreamscape and the more sophisticated style of *The Bends*, complete with passages of guitar noise that explode out of nowhere. Released in February 1993, on the B-side of 'Anyone Can Play Guitar', 'Coke Babies' is also known as "the song that ends with the sound of Colin Greenwood humming".

POP IS DEAD

MUCH abuse has been heaped on this leftover from *Pablo Honey* that had the unfortunate task of rescuing the band's career after the disappointing showing made by 'Anyone Can Play Guitar'. Partly a jibe at the build 'em up, knock 'em down nature of the business, and partly a genuinely jaundiced view of pop's tendency to eat itself, 'Pop Is Dead' itself seems to survive on rock'n'roll leftovers. At times, this sounds like a Mott The Hoople outtake. "A kind of epitaph of 1992," said Thom Yorke. Perhaps he meant to say 1972. Things could only get better...

BANANA CO (LIVE) CREEP (LIVE) RIPCORD (LIVE)

THREE live recordings propped up the May 1993 'Pop Is Dead' CD single. 'Banana Co' is a radio recording originally made for a local station in Cheshire; both 'Creep' and 'Ripcord' were taped live at the Town And Country Club in North London.

CREEP (ACOUSTIC)

THIS stripped back, solo acoustic take is hardly any less spine-tingling than the full band version, with Yorke's parting "I don't belong here" a poignant reminder of why he got into rock'n'roll in the first place. Ostensibly intended to bolster sales of 'Stop Whispering', the reappearance of Radiohead's best-known track made little difference in sales terms, and the single flopped.

YES I AM

IT'S GREAT sport spotting musical references where none was originally intended, but no one in the band would have missed the reworking of The Kinks' 'You Really Got Me' riff at the heart of 'Yes I Am'. More often overlooked, though, is the ambition inherent in the song. Starting quietly, in a manner not unlike Wire's 'Outdoor Miner', 'Yes I Am' builds with some subtlety before it climaxes in a baffling but nevertheless pleasing dual guitar battle that's part metal monster, part poodle rock. The song, which jabs a finger at music biz sycophants, was taped during the spring 1993 'Pop Is Dead' sessions with engineer Jim Warren, though eventually ended up on the flip of the reissued 'Creep' in the autumn.

INSIDE MY HEAD (LIVE)
YOU (LIVE)
VEGETABLE (LIVE)
KILLER CARS (LIVE)

THIS QUARTET of songs formed part of a set originally recorded for a radio broadcast at The Metro, Chicago on June 30, 1993. With 'Creep' getting the multi-formatting treatment in a bid to ensure it wouldn't fail a second time at home, these recordings provided a useful respite from the constant demands for new material. The various formats of the single also found room for a remix of 'Blow Out' from the first album, and the acoustic version of 'Creep' recorded at KROQ.

The *Bends* Era

THE TRICKSTER

"TRICKSTER is meaningless/Trickster is weak," Yorke sings midway through this, one of the more robust tracks spread across the 'My Iron Lung' formats. There's an affinity here with *Tinderbox*-era Siouxsie & The Banshees: the song undergoes several dramatic changes in pace, and there's even a moment when Thom Yorke attempts his best shot at a Siouxsie Sioux bellow.

PUNCHDRUNK LOVESICK SINGALONG

ONE OF Radiohead's most sophisticated early arrangements, its mellow atmosphere an echo of the fragile lyric, this song has been likened to Pink Floyd's slothful mournfulness. But there's at least as much Tim Buckley here, from the mouthful of a song title to the falsetto flourishes and the aching tenderness ("A beautiful girl can turn your world into dust"). Best of all, though, is the wonderfully subtle slide guitar that breaks up the verses. Of the many songs that were spread across the formats for 'My Iron Lung', this is probably the most impressive.

LOZENGE OF LOVE

NOT, apparently, a paean to Viagra, this turns out to be an impressive pastoral that finds Thom Yorke hitting impossibly high notes that would even leave the Buckleys gasping for breath. This improbably titled song begins like a tribute to George Harrison's raga-influenced 'Within You, Without You'. But what on the surface appears to be typical B-side fare does little justice to a song that, like much of the 'My Iron Lung' material, reveals a band desperate to leave the conformist sounds of *Pablo Honey* far behind. Incidentally, the title derives from a line in a Philip Larkin poem, *Sad Steps*.

LEWIS (MISTREATED)

DESCRIBED the mood of the 'My Iron Lung' sessions, producer John Leckie confessed that, "Being B-sides, of course, you don't want them to be too good. So we went

from trying to make a big hit to trying to make something not too great... That caused a lot of, 'What the fuck are we doing here?' kind of thoughts." That wasn't necessarily true. But while this jaw-jutting slice of pop advice to what seems to be a hapless work colleague too has its moments, especially before the bluster begins, it does largely bear out Leckie's assessment.

PERMANENT DAYLIGHT

TUCKED away on the second 'My Iron Lung' CD is this obvious nod to Sonic Youth. Yorke's spartan vocals are deliberately distorted, the guitars weave in and out of each other, and the *Daydream Nation* devotees must have been pleased with themselves. Though Radiohead never felt entirely comfortable aping the pre-grunge luminaries, the New Yorkers' unquenchable thirst for experimentation would soon prove just as much an inspiration.

YOU NEVER WASH UP AFTER YOURSELF

HAD THIS been written a few months later, this two-verse Thom Yorke solo fragment, taped at the band's rehearsal studio and issued on the second 'My Iron Lung' CD single in September 1994, would have been a candidate for the full 'Street Spirit' treatment. Full of melancholy, this single-take kitchen-sink micro-drama was written for a cast of one - Thom

Yorke during his difficult months back in 1993 – so it was probably best performed that way.

MAQUILADORA

IN LATIN AMERICA, *maquilaroda* is literally translated as 'assembly plant'. It's been suggested that this song is an early attack on multinational corporations, many of which have made huge inroads into Central and South America, where they guard their properties with military-like force. It's fitting, then, that 'Maquilaroda' begins with a Clash-like twin-guitar attack. It doesn't take long before this gives way to the kind of glam swagger associated with David Bowie's guitar-playing Spider From Mars, Mick Ronson. Located on the 'High And Dry' CD single, the impressive 'Maquiladora' is full of pompish bluster - and a nod in the direction of Phil Spector's 'Then He Kissed Me'.

PLANET TELEX
(HEXADECIMAL MIX)
PLANET TELEX (LFO JD MIX)
PLANET TELEX (KARMA
SUNRA VERSION)
PLANET TELEX (LIVE)

THE dramatic *Bends* opener remains the most remixed song in the Radiohead catalogue, with a chill-out Hexadecimal Mix and a rather more cut-up LFO JD Mix appearing on Discs One and Two of the 'High And Dry' single respectively. Further versions were spread across the 'Just' formats several

months later, in August 1995, with additional Also Mo' Wax and Trashed mixes appearing on various 'High And Dry' 12" releases too.

KILLER CARS

BRIEFLY considered as a follow-up to 'Creep', but ruled out because a live version had already been issued as part of the 'Creep' 12", 'Killer Cars' eventually surfaced in its studio form in February 1995 on the second 'High And Dry' CD single. Appearing in three different forms during the mid-Nineties, this song is undoubtedly a band favourite. The studio version is one of the first fruits of the liaison with John Leckie at RAK, in January 1994. The acoustic version, taped at the Metro in Chicago in June 1993, is perhaps a little too worthy, while the Mogadon Mix, on the first 'Just' CD, is – as one might predict – more moody.

INDIA RUBBER

WORKED into this song is a sampled, sped-up burst of Jonny Greenwood laughter, which is not inappropriate given its light, vaguely experimental style. Based around a simple drum groove – this was an early instance of the band's embrace with dance culture – 'India Rubber' boasts a weary, Dinosaur Jr-style chorus which, together with Yorke's sad clown motif, tends to undermine the surface cheeriness. 'India Rubber' appears on the first 'Fake Plastic Trees' CD.

HOW CAN YOU BE SURE?

RADIOHEAD'S penchant for traditional, acoustic-led rock balladry was most evident during their earliest years, though only once did they request the services of the obligatory female backing vocalist. Enter the unlikely named Dianne Swan. At its best, 'How Can You Be Sure?' has a late Sixties Stones' slothfulness about it ('Child Of The Moon', perhaps?). Less pleasingly, it also brings to mind a complacent, lighted-match Eighties stadium anthem. Another in Yorke's occasional 'What the hell are we doing together?' songs, this favourite of Colin Greenwood's was once considered for inclusion on *The Bends* before being shunted on to the flipside of 'Fake Plastic Trees'. The song did eventually find its way onto *The Bends* as a bonus track on the Japanese edition.

FAKE PLASTIC TREES (ACOUSTIC) BULLET PROOF... I WISH I WAS (ACOUSTIC) STREET SPIRIT (FADE OUT) (ACOUSTIC)

ACOUSTIC versions of three of the most notable tracks from *The Bends* were included on the second 'Fake Plastic Trees' CD single. All three were recorded live at Eve's Club in London, and feature just Thom and Jonny.

TALK SHOW HOST

THERE can be few more odious manifestations of everything that gets up Thom Yorke's nose than the ubiquitous all-talking, all-smiling, all-wisecracking talk show bore. Unsurprisingly, Radiohead are not regulars on the chat show circuit, give or take the odd 'intermission' song-only appearance. And Thom Yorke's claim here, "I want to be someone else or I'll explode", helps explain why. A sophisticated, trip-hop-influenced production recorded in the same three-day September 1995 sessions that yielded 'Lucky' and 'Bishop's Robes', 'Talk Show Host' initially appeared on the flip of the first 'Street Spirit' CD. The track was later remixed by Massive Attack associate Nellee Hooper for the soundtrack of *Romeo & Juliet*, and a Black Dog Remix appeared on *Foundations: Coming Up From The Streets* in 1997. With all that activity, it's hardly surprising that 'Talk Show Host' became a concert favourite – and one of the band's most cherished B-sides.

BONES ANYONE CAN PLAY GUITAR

THESE two songs, from *Pablo Honey* and *The Bends* respectively, appear in their live form on the flip of the second 'Just' CD single. Recorded live at the Forum, London, on 24 March 1995, both songs also turn up on *Live Au Forum*, a French-only release that same year, alongside live versions of 'Radio Telex' and 'Just'.

BISHOP'S ROBES

A DELICATE arrangement under-mines the indelicacy of this song's lyric, a fairly self-evident assassination of a "bastard head-master". Though Yorke has since insisted that the terrifying man in the bishop's robes was not a one-time headmaster of Abingdon School. However, his occasional on-stage comments ("The guy was a fascist idiot," he is reported to have once claimed), suggest that the song – which, oddly, is almost elega-ic – does have its roots in personal experience.

An early Nigel Godrich produc-tion, recorded at that memorable three-day stint in autumn 1995 together with 'Lucky' and 'Talk Show Host', 'Bishop's Robes' was issued on the flip of the 'Street Spirit' single. The song has a wonderful assur-ance about it, accentuated by slide guitar atmospherics, some neat Jonny Greenwood keyboards and a tambourine that sounds so cav-ernous that it could be from the first Velvet Underground album.

BANANA CO

O RIGINALLY released on the flip of 'Pop Is Dead', as an acoustic ver-sion taped for a local radio station, the song was finally given the full band treatment during the sum-mer 1994 sessions at The Manor. First issued on a compilation album,

Criminal Justice: Axe The Act, this fairly routine song subsequently appeared on the flipside of the sec-ond 'Street Spirit' CD.

MOLASSES

I T SOUNDS like a big, dreamy rock ballad was waiting to free itself from this track, but the band, with new producer Nigel Godrich at the controls, were hellbent on resisting it. The opening line, "Shake hands/ Genocide/Molasses", introduces global politics into Radiohead's scheme; Thom Yorke's self-harmon-ising is another innovation. Worked up during the summer of 1995, Molasses appeared in January 1996 on the second 'Street Spirit' CD.

The *OK Computer* Era

POLYETHYLENE (PARTS 1 & 2)

P ART 1', which merely consists of a single verse, features Thom Yorke, an acoustic guitar and more than a whiff of Beatles 'White Album' simplicity. By contrast, 'Part 2' veers off into the more complex world of Jethro Tull, Led Zeppelin and the first wave of stadium rock-ers, all jagged riffs and intricate structure. Yorke is at the top of his powers vocally, though, belting out snatched phrases from the heart of an antiseptic, health-obsessed cul-ture. This song could well have ended up on *OK Computer*, but instead found its way onto the first 'Paranoid Android' CD.

PEARLY*

UNUSUAL in that it's one of the few B-sides to feature – albeit intermittently - in Radiohead's live set, this dense, unrelenting attack on 'whiteness' ('Pearly' "runs from the Third World") was initially slated for inclusion on *OK Computer*, before being dropped and ending up on the flip of 'Paranoid Android'. There's some impressive Paul McCartney/Roger Waters-style attack from Colin Greenwood, while brother Jonny's guitar, which teeters on the edge of chaos throughout the song, bursts into glorious overload just as the fade begins. The asterisk is apparently part of the title, though no one has bothered to explain why.

A REMINDER

ANOTHER sometimes overlooked gem from the *OK Computer* sessions, 'A Reminder' begins with a slice-of-life recording taped in a train station in Prague, which eventually gives way to the disorientating sound of an echoing Fender Rhodes, and some disinterested, Velvet Underground-style strumming. Unsurprisingly, this lazy, dreamlike but undeniably beautiful song was written by Yorke on one of those 'do nothing' days on tour. On this particular day, he apparently sat and pondered on the perils of growing old. 'A Reminder' appears on the second 'Paranoid Android' CD.

MELATONIN

ANTICIPATING the atmospheric soundscapes of *Kid A*, this short drum and synth-strings piece reflects the cold, clinical matter of its title, named after a popular anti-ageing formula. Lyrically, the song is a meditation on parental love, with a fabulous black humour denouement, "Death to all who stand in your way". 'Melatonin' appears on the second 'Paranoid Android' CD single.

MEETING IN THE AISLE

APPEARING on the flip of the first 'Karma Police' CD, this was truly a taste of things to come, a programmed instrumental (the band's first) that pitches a repetitive guitar-swell against a complacent rhythm pattern, then muddies it with a mock-Eastern string sample. The effect is unsettling, in a 'bar music for a bar that's about to be bombed' kind of way.

LULL

THERE are moments when Radiohead appear to strive for the kind of near-telepathic musicality that was the hallmark of The Grateful Dead. But their songs are usually too structured, and anyway there's a residual fear of noodling that grips every band who claim at least some affinity to punk. But (almost certainly) unwittingly, the sound of the commune-dwelling West Coast legends finds it way into this apologetic *OK Computer*-era flipside. Jonny Greenwood's xylophone and the delightful guitar arpeggio that accompanies it are amusingly reminiscent of 'New Potato Caboose' on the Dead's 1968 classic, *Anthem Of The Sun*. Double fun, then, when elsewhere on the song, Thom Yorke delivers one line ("I'm sorry that I lost control") in the heartfelt manner of Jerry Garcia on 1971's 'Wharf Rat'. 'Lull' can be found on the flip of the first 'Karma Police' CD.

CLIMBING UP THE WALLS (ZERO 7 MIX)
CLIMBING UP THE WALLS (FILA BRAZILLIA MIX)

CLUB-BOUND remixes of one of the weaker tracks on *OK Computer*, these rip out its heart and put an overpriced bottle of beer in its hand. It's difficult to imagine many enthusiasts ripping open their brand new copy of the second 'Karma Police' CD with as much enthusiasm as the first.

PALO ALTO

THE self-styled "city of the future", its growth largely down to ex-hippies who got into technology, Palo Alto lies in the heart of Silicone Valley in California. Radiohead stopped off there in 1996 to marvel at its achievements (and pay homage to the famed Apple computer headquarters). Thom Yorke appears to channel his thoughts on the matter here with wonderful, if surprising restraint, raising at least one black laugh with the line, "It's amazing/I'm killing myself for someone else". The key line, though, is "I'm OK, how are you?", an extension of the dehumanising meaning behind *OK Computer*.

Not quite good enough to be regarded as the missing link between *OK Computer* and *Kid A*, this flipside turns up on the first 'No Surprises' CD single.

HOW I MADE MY MILLIONS

A ONE-man-and-his-piano home demo, recorded while Yorke's (clearly audible) girlfriend washes dishes in the kitchen close by. The aura of John and Yoko-like domesticity is echoed by the song's acutely reflective mood, though 'Imagine' this isn't. The piano's hardly up to Lennon's posh, pure white grand, and while the ex-Beatle repeats his message of hope, Thom Yorke prefers to "Let it fall". This amusingly titled song eventually found its way onto the first 'No Surprises' CD single.

AIRBAG (LIVE)

THIS impressive stab at an obviously studio-enhanced song was recorded in Florence on October 30, 1997, and became an extra on the second 'No Surprises' CD at the start of 1998.

LUCKY (LIVE)

THE second live track on the second 'No Surprises' disc was recorded in Berlin on November 3, 1997. Inevitably, a little of the song's majestic beauty gets lost in translation, but the dynamics still work impressively well in the live arena.

The *Amnesiac* Era

THE AMAZING SOUND OF ORGY

IMAGINE: PJ Harvey and David (*Twin Peaks*) Lynch's favourite composer Angelo Badalamenti in a room and forced to collaborate on a song for Thom Yorke. The results wouldn't be far from this marvellous muddle of jazz shuffle and voodoo blues, with a generous serving of extraterrestrial sounds for good measure. Titled after a little-known US nu-metal band, 'The Amazing Sound Of Orgy' serves up a worthy side-dish on the 'Pyramid Song' CD.

TRANS-ATLANTIC DRAWL

FOR 90 SECONDS, this pumps out aggressive anarcho-rock, as if sessions for Nirvana's *In Utero* had been invaded by an alien trying to imitate Macy Gray. Enough bizarre behaviour for one song, you might think. But one savage edit later, the noise abates and is crudely replaced by what sounds like a sonic interpretation of a difficult, distorted afterlife. It's not a bad indication of

Yorke's rhetorical question earlier in the song: "Do you see light at the end of the tunnel?" You'll find this idiosyncratic – even by Radiohead standards – track on the 'Pyramid Song' CD.

FAST-TRACK

BACK in March 2000, Ed O'Brien recorded in his online diary that Thom Yorke had been "singing along" to this new song. The singer obviously had second thoughts because, by the time it appeared on the second 'Pyramid Song' CD, 'Fast-Track' had become an instrumental electro-collage.

KINETIC

ONCE again, we turn to Ed O'Brien's online diary for enlightenment: "Jonny and I are let loose on fucking up Phil's drum sound," he wrote during sessions for this 'Pyramid Song' CD add-on. Competing with the percussive disorder (which, some say, includes a Miles Davis sample) is a distracting synthesized backing vocal part, reminiscent of Laurie Anderson's 'O Superman', that has the rare distinction of virtually eclipsing Yorke's lyric contribution. (It's difficult to miss a recurrence of his favourite theme, though: "Don't fall asleep at the wheel".)

WORRYWORT

WE'RE back into *Kid A/ Amnesiac*-style territory, with

Thom Yorke convincing himself that "it's such a beautiful day" against a backdrop of gentle keyboard rhythms, which eventually builds into something that might be described as restrained cacophony. If that appeals, then look no further than the second CD issue of 'Knives Out'.

FOG

ONE OF the very best-kept secrets in the Radiohead canon, this started life as a turn-of-the-century piano-piece titled 'Alligators In New York Sewers'. By the time it appeared on the 'Knives Out' CD, (Fog) had been transformed into an extraordinary and unique ensemble piece. It's short on convention but wonderfully long and panoramic in terms of atmosphere. Distorted bass and gentle tambourine set the parameters, a recurring keyboard motif provides an ever-present drip-drip of creepiness, while Thom Yorke adds to the horror film scenario with a lyric about trapped children and monsters waiting to pounce – or our freedoms fast being snatched away, if you prefer.

CUTTOOTH

A PROMINENT piano, a la The Rolling Stones' 'Let's Spend The Night Together', provides the engine on this insistent addition to the 'Knives Out' CD. Once wrongly identified as 'Tongue-Tied', because of its chorus line, this impressive track finds Yorke dipping into a few

familiar themes – escape, oppression, helplessness. This track will gain its rightful place in the Radiohead hall of fame when Parlophone sees fit to eclipse the internet compilers and release that inevitable B-sides collection.

LIFE IN A GLASSHOUSE (FULL VERSION)

YES, extra-strength Humphrey Lyttleton and his band of trumpeteers, for the second 'Knives Out' CD, an experience followed by the video for the title track.

The *Hail To The Theif* Era

PAPERBAG WRITER

IT'S NOT a great title – though it could have been worse: 'Hey Dude', anyone? – but it does amplify the ever-present spectre of The Beatles throughout the band's career. The song's key refrain – "Blow into this paper bag" – invokes the drunk driver, in the light of Yorke's acute interest in road safety, not necessarily an admirable character. This song turns up as a B-side of 'There There'.

WHERE BLUEBIRDS FLY

BLUEBIRDS appear to fly on the extended 'There There' CD, where there is a beguiling backdrop of high-speed computer game cacophony and stately keyboard moves – and very little evidence of Dorothy or *The Wizard of Oz*, as the title might suggest. Anyone not happily settled before hearing this track certainly won't be afterwards. This instrumental track was regularly used as the intro music during the band's 2002/2003 tours.

I AM CITIZEN INSANE

IF THE FALL'S Mark E. Smith can proclaim himself 'I Am Damo Suzuki', then Thom Yorke can surely restyle himself after Orson Welles' 1941 masterpiece on the corrupting nature of power and the media. But, unlike The Fall's majestic effort, Yorke fails to rise to the occasion here, with this woozy techno instrumental sounding tired, lacking direction and sorely in need of inspiration from a muse who might or might not be named Rosebud. You'll find 'I Am Citizen Insane' on the first 'Go To Sleep' CD.

FOG (AGAIN) LIVE

THIS minimalist, piano and voice reinterpretation of the trance-like 'Knives Out' B-side was taped live in Paris on July 3, 2003. Once described by Thom Yorke as "a silly song", 'Fog' sounds quite beautiful here, more akin to a cerebral lullaby. And that's despite a lyric that seems to lament the corruption of children who "grow up so fast". "How did you go bad?" asks Yorke. As an aside, it's not difficult to envisage how this stripped-down song, issued on the flip of the first 'Go To Sleep' CD, might

sound in the hands of The Verve.

GAGGING ORDER

PERHAPS all those hillside walks in East Dorset while working up material for *Hail To The Thief* inspired Yorke to write this pastoral for voice and finger-picked solo guitar. A raw performance pockmarked with guitar buzz and occasionally awkward picking, 'Gagging Order' is hardly among his most enchanting melodies, though it's pleasant enough. In 'White Album' terms, the song – issued on the flip of the second 'Go To Sleep' CD - is roughly the equivalent of 'Mother Nature's Son'.

I AM A WICKED CHILD

A RARE Radiohead excursion into the blues that finds the band encroaching on PJ Harvey territory – without nearly the same conviction, it must be said. Jonny Greenwood's filthy harmonica turn is the stand-out element here, in a performance that's as loose as anything the band has yet released. 'I Am A Wicked Child' can be found on the second 'Go To Sleep' CD.

REMYXOMATOSIS (CHRISTIAN VOGEL REMIX)

'MYXOMATOSIS' was one of the high points of *Hail To The Thief*, but it loses much in the remixing for the flip of the '2+2=5' single, not least its lunatic bass line. Starved of its key attributes, 'Remyxomatosis' is transformed into something considerably less unique, though Vogel's sound effects and percussive tweaks do lend the piece a different kind of urgency.

THERE THERE (DEMO)

A WORKING version of one of the band's key songs, this leads off with a thinner, Can-style percussive beat, here brought right to the fore. A ragged, fuzzed-up guitar part indicates that this is an early version, and though Thom Yorke's melody is already in place, there is no evidence of the secondary voices that brought so much to the finished version. But even a half-hearted run through one of Radiohead's most intoxicating tracks is a thrill, and while this doesn't yet hit the peaks of the finished single, it boasts a longer outro that seems to shift from Can to early Cabaret Voltaire for inspiration. This enlightening demo appears on the '2+2=5' CD.

SKTTRBRAIN (FOUR TET REMIX)

H ARDLY a highlight of *Hail To The Thief*, 'Scatterbrain' has much less to lose from a Four Tet remix, which brings a mix of horns and minimalism to Yorke's mournful melody. Find it on the flip of the second '2+2=5' single.

I WILL (LA MIX)

T HE ORIGINAL mix of the *Hail To The Thief* song, as first recorded at Ocean Way in LA, rounds off the second '2+2=5' CD. While it's busier than the album version, it's not necessarily better.

2. Tracks on Compilations

R ADIOHEAD HAVE DONATED COUNTLESS ALTERNATE TAKES AND LIVE RECORDINGS to compilation albums. Among the most notable is the demo version of '(Nice Dream)', with altered lyrics, which can be found on *Volume 13*, issued in 1995. Another song from *The Bends*, a September 1994 Radio 1 Evening Sessions version of 'Street Spirit', turned up on *Hold On: BBC Radio 1FM Sessions*. Meanwhile, a version of 'Just', recorded live at Glastonbury in 1994, turned up on *The Radio1FM Sessions* CD, cover-mounted with *Vox* magazine. A live version of 'Paranoid Android', taped at Glastonbury in 1997, was a highlight on *Mud For It: Glastonbury '97*, while another live festival recording, 'Fake Plastic Trees' taped on June 15, 1998, can be heard on the *Tibetan Freedom Concert* album. That same song also turns up in a live-for-MTV version on MTV's *120 Minutes Live*, while another Tibet-related release, the *Long Live Tibet* compilation, includes a four-track demo version of 'The Bends'. The 'Subterranean Homesick Alien' that turns up on *Rare On Air: Volume 4*, features Thom and Jonny performing an acoustic version for radio. More recently, a demo of 'Where I End And You Begin' turned up on *The Big Noise*, a CD freebie with *The Guardian* newspaper in 2003.

3. Imports

AN ENTIRE BOOK COULD BE WRITTEN ON THE VARIOUS PERMUTATIONS ON offer at the Radiohead import counter. However, mention should be made here of a small handful that include otherwise unavailable material, almost invariably live recordings.

A French 'Creep' EP, issued in 1994, augmented the studio version of the song with three live cuts, 'The Bends', 'Prove Yourself' and 'Creep', performed at The Black Session on February 23, 1993. Two years later, another French EP boasted of three songs, 'My Iron Lung', 'Just' and 'Maquiladora', recorded at the Astoria show on 27 May 1994.

Holland is an important market for seeking out stray live recordings. A 1996 CD, *2 Meter Session*, includes versions of 'Street Spirit', 'Anyone Can Play Guitar' and 'Bones', recorded at the Melkweg, while the Dutch edition of 'My Iron Lung' includes an additional take of that song recorded at Rock City, Nottingham. More material from that show appear on the so-called *Pinkpop* EP, issued free with early copies of *The Bends* in Holland and Belgium. Featured songs are 'Fake Plastic Trees', 'Blow Out', 'Bones', 'You' and 'High And Dry', though some pressings play a live '(Nice Dream)' instead of 'You'. More recently, another *Pinkpop* EP included live versions of 'The National Anthem' and 'Idioteque', recorded in Dublin in 2000.

While useful in gathering up many of the B-sides from the *OK Computer* era, *Running From Demons*, a Japan-only EP from 1997, also includes a previously unheard remix of 'Pearly*'.

In 2004, a live version of '2+2=5', recorded at Earls Court, London on November 26, 2003, turned up on *Com Lag: 2+2=5*, initially compiled for the Japanese market but subsequently released in other territories. A ten-track collection of *Hail To The Thief* flipsides, it follows in the wake of the *My Iron Lung* and *Airbag/How Am I Driving?* B-side collections.

4. Collaborations & Guest Appearances

UNSURPRISINGLY, **THOM YORKE HAS BEEN THE MOST PROLIFIC BAND MEMBER** away from Radiohead. One of his first extra-curricular activities was to record a duet with Isabel Monteiro for the 1998 Drugstore single, 'El President'. The song can also be found on the band's *White Magic For Lovers* album. Around the same time, Yorke turned up singing Pink Floyd's 'Wish You Were Here' down a phone line for Sparklehorse. The cover duly appeared on a compilation album, *Come Again*.

Most suggestive of Radiohead's soon to be revealed new direction was the tie-up with UNKLE, the James Lavelle project also featuring DJ Shadow. The resulting 'Rabbit In Your Headlights' was issued on single (and in several mixes too), and also turned up on the 1998 UNKLE album, *Psyence Fiction*.

Around the time of *Kid A*, two further collaborations appeared that seemed to confirm Yorke's tendency to make new alliances with rock's more outré musicians. 'I've Seen It All', his duet with Bjork, was recorded for the soundtrack of her stunning film appearance, *Dancer In The Dark*, and can be found on her album, *Selmasongs*. He spent even more time with PJ Harvey, recording a duet, 'This Mess We're In', and contributing backing vocals to two other songs, 'Beautiful Feeling' and 'One Line', all from her award-winning album from 2000, *Stories From The City, Stories From The Sea*.

More recently, he teamed up as part of the all-star Band Aid 2004 for the revival of the 1984 charity hit, 'Do They Know It's Christmas?'

Both Thom Yorke and Jonny Greenwood performed incognito as part of a fictional band, The Venus In Furs, for the soundtrack of the Michael Stipe-produced 1998 glam-rock movie, *Velvet Goldmine*. Also in the line-up were ex-Suede guitarist Bernard Butler and original Roxy Music sax player Andy Mackay, the latter lending authenticity to the three Roxy covers, '2HB', 'Ladytron' and 'Bitter-Sweet'. The 'Venus In Furs' also tackled Eno's 'Baby's On Fire' and a fifth song, 'Tumbling Down'.

The Roxy Music connection was furthered in 2003 when Jonny Greenwood guested on 'Hiroshima', a track on Bryan Ferry's *Frantic*. The guitarist's other notable guest appearance was in 1998, when he played harmonica on two songs ('Platform Blues' and 'Billie') on Pavement's *Terror Twilight* album, produced by Nigel Godrich.

Most notably, Jonny Greenwood is the only band member to have released a solo album, *Bodysong* (EMI; 2003). A richly textured film soundtrack that blends an eclectic mix of classical, jazz, ambient, folk and electronica, it is unsurprisingly short on guitar-playing.

Phil Selway and Ed O'Brien guest on Neil Finn & Friends' 2001 album, 7 *Worlds Collide*, while Ed later teamed up with Asian Dub Foundation for 'Enemy Of The Enemy', issued in 2003.

DVD/Video

FOUR RADIOHEAD FILMS HAVE SO FAR BEEN MADE AVAILABLE. *THE ASTORIA London Live: 27 May 1995* is an hour-long-plus concert movie that captures the band in concert just weeks after the release of *The Bends*. This is the show where the backing track for 'My Iron Lung' was recorded.

Considerably more artful on every level is 7 *Television Commercials*, a dryly named 1998 collection of promo videos for 'Paranoid Android', 'Street Spirit', 'No Surprises', 'Just', 'High And Dry', 'Karma Police' and 'Fake Plastic Trees'.

Grant Gee's *Meeting People Is Easy*, issued in 1999, is a full-length documentary filmed in the goldfish bowl that was the *OK Computer* tour. In addition to providing an insight into the media circus that that unfolds when a rock band rides into town, the film captures the band's slow disintegration on the road. It also features excerpts from 16 songs (shot at gigs in Barcelona, Paris, New York and Tokyo), including tantalising glimpses of the band working on material that would later turn up on *Kid A* and *Amnesiac*.

The latest release is certainly the most provocative yet. Titled *The Most Gigantic Lying Mouth Of All Time*, this self-styled "110 minute excursion into the bizarre" features 24 short films originally put together for Radiohead Television, with a view to a terrestrial broadcast. That never happened, so the melange of lo-fi footage (some shot by the band, other clips donated by fans), promo videos, *Hail To The Thief*-era music and the deranged introductions of one Chieftan Mews, was made available in December 2004 via the group's website instead.

Index